Institute of Leadership
& Management

superseries

Understanding Organizations in their Context

FIFTH EDITION

Published for the
Institute of Leadership & Management

ELSEVIER

AMSTERDAM • BOSTON • HEIDELBERG • LONDON • NEW YORK • OXFORD
PARIS • SAN DIEGO • SAN FRANCISCO • SINGAPORE • SYDNEY • TOKYO
Pergamon Flexible Learning is an imprint of Elsevier

Pergamon
Flexible
Learning

Pergamon Flexible Learning is an imprint of Elsevier
Linacre House, Jordan Hill, Oxford OX2 8DP, UK
30 Corporate Drive, Suite 400, Burlington, MA 01803, USA

First edition 1986
Second edition 1991
Third edition 1997
Fourth edition 2003
Fifth edition 2007

Editor: David Pardey

Based on material in previous editions of this work

The views expressed in this work are those of the authors and do
not necessarily reflect those of the Institute of Leadership &
Management or of the publisher

Notice
No responsibility is assumed by the publisher for any injury and/or damage to persons or
property as a matter of products liability, negligence or otherwise, or from any use or operation
of any methods, products, instructions or ideas contained in the material herein

British Library Cataloguing in Publication Data
A catalogue record for this book is available from the British Library

Library of Congress Cataloguing in Publication Data
A catalogue record for this book is available from the Library of Congress

ISBN 978-0-08-046427-5

For information on all Pergamon Flexible Learning publications
visit our website at http://books.elsevier.com

Institute of Leadership & Management
Registered Office
1 Giltspur Street
London
EC1A 9DD
Telephone: 020 7294 2470
www.i-l-m.com
ILM is part of the City & Guilds Group

Typeset by Charon Tec Ltd (A Macmillan Company), Chennai, India
www.charontec.com
Printed and bound in Great Britain

07 08 09 10 11   10 9 8 7 6 5 4 3 2 1

Working together to grow
libraries in developing countries

www.elsevier.com | www.bookaid.org | www.sabre.org

ELSEVIER   BOOK AID
International   Sabre Foundation

Contents

Series preface   vii

Unit specification   ix

Workbook introduction   xi

1   ILM Super Series study links   xi

2   Links to ILM qualifications   xi

3   Workbook objectives   xi

Session A   Why organizations need to exist   1

1   Introduction   1

2   What organizations are for   2

3   Is there 'an organization for all purposes'?   3

4   Types of organization   7

5   Organizational structures   21

6   Organizational functions   32

7   Summary   36

Session B   The need for accounts   37

1   Introduction   37

2   How money is used   37

3   The use of accounting records   39

4   Accounting records and accounts   46

5   How a business works   50

6   Cash flow   56

7   Summary   66

Contents

Session C Financial information   67

   1   Introduction   67
   2   Cash accounting versus profit accounting   67
   3   The profit and loss account   69
   4   The balance sheet   75
   5   Financial indicators   85
   6   Summary   95

Session D Sources of finance   97

   1   Introduction   97
   2   Funds available   97
   3   Short-term finance   98
   4   Medium-term and long-term finance   100
   5   Flexible financing   103
   6   Summary   105

Session E The economic environment   107

   1   Introduction   107
   2   How economics affects everyone   110
   3   Factors of production   112
   4   Raw materials   117
   5   The price mechanism   121
   6   The economic levers which governments use   131
   7   Key economic issues affecting all organizations   139
   8   Summary   148

Session F The global village   149

   1   Introduction   149
   2   The UK's international trade   150
   3   The UK's trading partners   155
   4   The European Union (EU)   161
   5   International organizations which influence the UK   166
   6   The trade cycle, unemployment and economic growth   172
   7   Summary   179

Performance checks 181

1   Quick quiz   181
2   Workbook assessment   185

Reflect and review 187

1   Reflect and review   187
2   Action plan   190
3   Extensions   192
4   Answers to self-assessment questions   198
5   Answers to activities   205
6   Answers to the quick quiz   211
7   Certificate   213

Series preface

Whether you are a tutor/trainer or studying management development to further your career, Super Series provides an exciting and flexible resource to help you to achieve your goals. The fifth edition is completely new and up-to-date, and has been structured to perfectly match the Institute of Leadership & Management (ILM)'s new unit-based qualifications for first line managers. It also harmonizes with the 2004 national occupational standards in management and leadership, providing an invaluable resource for S/NVQs at Level 3 in Management.

Super Series is equally valuable for anyone tutoring or studying any management programmes at this level, whether leading to a qualification or not. Individual workbooks also support short programmes, which may be recognized by ILM as Endorsed or Development Awards, or provide the ideal way to undertake CPD activities.

For learners, coping with all the pressures of today's world, Super Series offers you the flexibility to study at your own pace to fit around your professional and other commitments. You don't need a PC or to attend classes at a specific time – choose when and where to study to suit yourself! And you will always have the complete workbook as a quick reference just when you need it.

For tutors/trainers, Super Series provides an invaluable guide to what needs to be covered, and in what depth. It also allows learners who miss occasional sessions to 'catch up' by dipping into the series.

Super Series provides unrivalled support for all those involved in first line management and supervision.

Unit specification

Title:	Understanding organizations in their context	Unit Ref:	M3.24
Level:	3		
Credit value:	2		

Learning outcomes *The learner* will		Assessment criteria *The learner* can *(in an organization with which the learner is familiar)*	
1. Understand the context within which an organization operates	1.1 1.2 1.3 1.4 1.5	Identify the legal entity of the organization List the operational functions within the organization Use an organizational chart to identify own role, span of control and reporting line in the organization Briefly outline the roles and responsibilities of managers at different levels of the organization Briefly explain the relevance to an organization of its different stakeholders	
2. Understand the financial environment within which an organization operates	2.1 2.2 2.3 2.4	Explain the importance of financial information for management Identify the main financial documents needed by the organization and briefly describe the information they contain Identify the most significant financial indicators of business performance in the organization and briefly describe their relevance List the main sources of long, medium and short-term funds for the organization	
3. Understand the economic environment within which an organization operates	3.1 3.2	Identify the major economic and political forces which impact upon the organization Briefly describe how government attempts to influence the economy and its effect on the organization's operations	

Workbook introduction

 1 ILM Super Series study links

This workbook addresses the issues of *Understanding Organizations in their Context*. Should you wish to extend your study to other Super Series workbooks covering related or different subject areas, you will find a comprehensive list at the back of this book.

 2 Links to ILM qualifications

This workbook relates to the learning outcomes of Unit M3.24 Understanding organizations in their context from the ILM Level 3 Award, Certificate and Diploma in First Line Management.

 3 Workbook objectives

All of us deal with organizations large and small every day of the year. One organization collects the rubbish regularly, another supplies water, another runs the shops and others provide the daily necessities of life. Organizations educate children, care for the sick, serve charitable causes, and provide entertainment, car servicing, public transport, and the goods and services that people expect to be available in a modern society. Unless you live on a desert island, you simply cannot get away from organizations.

Most of the people reading this book work for an organization in the public or private sector of the United Kingdom's massive economy. This is presided over, to some degree, by a government which itself is a massive organization. But are all organizations much the same? Should they all have the same basic structures? Or are there different kinds of organization that are best suited to achieving particular objectives? This is the question we will try to answer in this workbook.

As a line manager, you may be involved in the production or sale of goods, or delivery of services. Your performance at work, along with that of our work team, determines how well your organization does financially and how successful it is. Whether you work in a business that sets out to make a profit, or in the voluntary sector, your organization is interested in making the best use of the funds it has available. And those who supply the funds, whether they are shareholders, partners or individuals making donations, are keen to see that their money is well used. They obtain that information from year-end financial statements such as a company's annual published report and accounts.

Management also needs financial information to help it run the organization day to day, and specific accounts are prepared for its use too. In this workbook, we will look at what is included in these accounts, what they tell us and how they are used. We'll explore the way money is used in a business, and look at how performance can be measured in financial terms. Financial constraints are often very important to organizations; developing your understanding of finances will help you improve your effectiveness in the workplace. You will spot ways in which money can be better used.

Accountancy, like all specialist subjects, has its own language. Just as a car mechanic will talk of 'torque' and 'gaskets', and a computer expert will discuss 'bytes' and 'disk access time', an accountant uses expressions such as 'current liabilities' and 'retained profit'. By the end of this workbook, you will have a better appreciation of accounting vocabulary and this, in itself, will clarify what is meant by aspects of accounts that you may have found confusing and mysterious in the past.

As well as looking at the financial context of the organization, we will also examine its economic context. Like accountancy, economics has its own specialists language which hides the fact that practical people the world over understand the basics of economics. A cocoa farmer in West Africa, an English supplier of table lamps to major retailers and the champagne growers of France all understand intuitively the basic economic facts of life. They experience them from day to day and from season to season – just go to any market place anywhere in the country and you will see economic market forces in action. Economics has an unenviable reputation for being the 'gloomy science', full of concepts unintelligible to anyone other than specialists. In that respect it is no different from the technical specialisms of everybody reading this book. Economists would be just as lost in the jargon jungles of computing, telecommunications, customer relations management, operating theatre practice or risk management unless someone were kind enough to provide them with some guidance.

This book is intended to do just that, and to be an enduring reference work for the basics. As with all complex structures, the economic systems of the UK, the EU and the global economy rest on simple structures which are perfectly intelligible to anyone and everyone. There is nothing to fear in the study of the economic environment in which your organization works. It is relevant to everything that you do – and is easier to grasp in principle than many complex technical and managerial tasks which you face every day in your normal working life.

3.1 Objectives

When you have completed this workbook you will be better able to:

- describe the forms that organizations can take, the functions required to maintain them, and the proper roles of managers at various levels within them;
- distinguish between different organizational structures and their 'fitness for purpose' in differing situations;
- understand how important it is for any organization to have sufficient cash;
- appreciate why it is vital for an organization to control its finances by forecasting and monitoring cash flow;
- identify appropriate providers of finance in given situations;
- make sense of key financial information in profit and loss accounts and balance sheets;
- measure how well an organization is performing financially;
- list the fundamental factors of production and be able to relate them to your own organization and everyday working life;
- outline the eternal economic problems and the limited range of political measures available to tackle them;
- recognize the important economic and political factors which affect your organization;
- explain the effect of currency exchange rates on organizations in all countries;
- describe the structure of the EU and its impact EU on the UK and its business;
- identify the influences beyond the EU which are significant for UK business;
- outline the effect which the globalization of business has on local organizations throughout the world.

Session A
Why organizations need to exist

1 Introduction

'They couldn't organize a booze-up in a brewery' is typical of the derogatory comments that are made frequently about unsuccessful activity in every walk of life – from sport to politics, and from high-level business to the local horticultural society or social club.

The signs of disorganization are easy enough to recognize – people rushing around, often working very hard individually, but achieving little collectively.

If, then, the signs of disorganization are obvious to anyone, what should you observe when an organization is 'well run'?

Activity 1

From your own experience as a customer, as a user of public services, entertainment and sport, jot down as many signs as you can that an organization is working *smoothly*.

_____

_____

_____

Your answers probably all said in effect that, when an organization works smoothly, you hardly notice it is there at all. For example:

■ the corps de ballet dance in unison, the players in an orchestra play their assigned parts in tune and on the beat, and the actors in a stage play know their lines and speak them 'in turn' as written by the author;
■ the players in a football, hockey, basketball or netball team seem to know 'instinctively' where the ball should be despatched to next;
■ the shelves of the local shop are stocked with all the 'best-selling items', and the mail order company delivers your order on time and in good condition;
■ a fire engine arrives promptly in response to a '999' call and the crew know where the hydrants are, how to use the equipment and get on with the job, with little need for the officer in charge to say anything.

People often use phrases like 'running on oiled wheels' to describe the tangible effects of good organization. But, as you will know from experience, good organization in the managerial context does not just happen. It involves a great deal of hard work 'behind the scenes'.

All the above examples of good organization involve teams of people working towards a common purpose. The individuals within these teams may or may not be well organized on a personal level. However, if they are well organized, their collective talents, experience and goodwill can be wasted by a badly structured organization, or a well structured one that is badly run.

2 What organizations are for

If any organization is to be worth having, then the result it achieves should be such that:

'the whole is greater than the sum of its parts'.

What this means, in practice, is that the combined effect of the individual elements support and enable each to perform to its maximum capability. Given that these 'elements' are, primarily, people, this depends on:

■ how worthwhile the organization's purpose is perceived to be by the majority of its staff;
■ how well its structure is designed to accommodate the individual talents they possess;
■ how well it is managed at every level.

All three elements need to be present for any organization to function well. They are like the legs of a three-legged stool. Remove any one of the legs and the stool will collapse under its own weight, before any external pressure is applied.

3 Is there 'an organization for all purposes'?

'Organization' is used in common speech as though it has a single meaning, but is that true? Is there a single organizational structure which will work for all purposes?

Activity 2 ·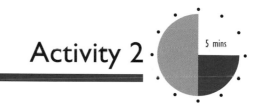

5 mins

Imagine you are asked to set up a number of organizations to achieve the following purposes:

- to buy specialist goods from North Africa and the Middle East and sell them entirely via the Internet;
- to raise money for a charity via a chain of shops, 90% of whose workers will be unpaid;
- to organize a celebration for the 50th anniversary of the local tennis club;
- to supply electricity to the whole of a UK region, comprising 20,000 square miles, 2 million households, plus a mix of large industrial and commercial users;
- to research into finding improved methods of treating a rare debilitating disease.

What differences, if any, do you think there should be between the structures of the organizations you set up? Jot down your ideas.

_____

_____

_____

_____

_____

_____

Compare your own thoughts with the following about suitable structures to serve these widely differing purposes.

- An organization buying goods from a number of countries, and selling them on the Internet, would require a network of contacts in the countries involved, some of them fluent in the languages spoken. It would also require expertise in designing and operating websites and ensuring that everyone gets paid. It would need to be flexible, to cope with varying supply and demand for the products.
- Managing mainly unpaid volunteers requires a very different approach to, for example, the structure that would work for a commercial retailer. Lines of communication need to be kept short and the volunteers must be chosen for their commitment to the charity's purpose and reminded constantly *why* they subscribe to it.
- For a 'one-off' purpose, such as organizing a celebration, the need is for an informal group of self-motivated people who are committed to the task and can bring different skills and experience to bear upon it – for example, one who is familiar with the club's history, another who can publicize the event and help put that history into pictures and words, another who can deal with raising and accounting for any money required and another with expertise and/or contacts in catering. All must be prepared to work without pay and discipline themselves to attend meetings and carry out the tasks which they agree to undertake with minimal – or no – supervision.

Many organizations try to make their purpose clear through a mission statement. There is an example in EXTENSION 1.

- A massive undertaking, such as supplying electricity to a whole UK region, has huge safety health and social implications. It requires a formal structure, staffed by competent specialists who react to virtually any circumstance – from bad weather to terrorism – and develop tremendous technical and administrative expertise.
- Intensive research would demand the use of original thinkers and highly individual experts, who would almost certainly resent the rigid structure required to supply electricity. Some of them might need to be paid more highly than managers more senior to them in the organization in 'hierarchical' terms, to attract the calibre of specialist required.

The workable organizational structures that have evolved over the centuries have taken their basic **purpose** as their starting point. Where problems arise it is because:

- the organization's purpose is ill-defined, or has changed over time;
- a structure inappropriate to the purpose has been imposed;
- the people who work in the organization have not been convinced that they should support the organization's purpose, and/or resent a structure that they find either too rigid or too unsupportive.

Various combinations of these ills are possible, and ailing organizations frequently suffer from all three.

The Millennium Dome was built on reclaimed industrial land with some £0.5 billion capital funding from the National Lottery. The New Millennium Experience Company (NMEC), which built it, was a public company with a single share owned by a Minister, initially Peter Mandelson and subsequently Lord Falconer. Its Board was chaired by Bob Ayling (of British Airways) and contained politicians, business people and figures from the arts and entertainment industries. Its first chief executive, Jennie Page, was seconded from the Civil Service but she resigned halfway through the year because of the financial difficulties NMEC faced. Her replacement (Frenchman Pierre Yves Gerbeau) was recruited from Disneyland Paris.

The Dome was part of a wider economic development on the Greenwich peninsular, including new housing and improved transport infrastructure. The major problem for the Dome was that it was never quite clear whether it was educational or for entertainment – a science and culture exhibition or a theme park, reflecting the fundamentally Christian nature of the millennium or the multi-faith nature of the UK today. To complicate matters further, the high profile involvement of a government meant that it took on a highly symbolic status, so that its success or failure was seen by many government critics as indicative of its general competence.

Added to this, according to a National Audit Office report, the Millennium Dome was badly managed, its visitor number target of 12 million was 'ambitious and inherently risky' and it was 'clear that the task of managing the project had been complicated by the complex organizational arrangements put in place from the outset, and by the failure to put in sufficiently robust financial management'. The NMEC had 'weaknesses in financial management and control' and it had been unable to 'track and quantify fully the contractual commitments it has entered into'. The company 'experienced difficulty in establishing the full extent of its liabilities through to solvent liquidation and handover to a new owner'.

In response to these comments, Lord Falconer said: '… we should not lose sight of what has been achieved. The dome is the number one pay-to-visit attraction in the UK, with over 5.4 m visits so far – with visitor satisfaction ratings among the industry's highest'.

Activity 3 · 5 mins

Think back to the three-legged stool and describe briefly where you see signs of potential failure with any of its legs in the case of the Millennium Dome.

■ Purpose

_____

_____

■ Appropriate structure

_____

_____

■ Managerial competence

_____

_____

You almost certainly identified cracks in all three 'legs'.

■ **Purpose**
It was very unclear what the Millennium Dome's main purpose was. Was it an engine of economic and social development on the Greenwich peninsular, or was the site chosen for political reasons? Was it to attract overseas visitors, or was it primarily for UK citizens? Was it to inform or entertain?

■ **Structure**
The Dome was a complicated operation, requiring large numbers of people, first to build it and then to operate it. The management of a construction business is always going to be different from that of a 'visitor attraction' and this inevitably put pressure on its organizational ability. According to the NAO its 'complex organizational arrangements' suggest that it was poorly structured to achieve its purpose – whatever that was! Furthermore, the politicized nature of the Dome, its mixture of Board members from business, arts, entertainment and politics, was always likely to lead to conflicts.

■ **Managerial competence**
The NAO was highly critical of the management of the Dome with criticisms of its 'failure to put in sufficiently robust financial management' and 'weaknesses in financial management and control', its inability 'to track and quantify

> The Millennium Dome closed at the end of the year 2000, and has remained empty and unused at the time of writing, six years later. Its continuing embarrassment to the government emphasizes the failure to be clear about the long-term as well as the short-term purpose of the building.

fully (its) contractual commitments' and its 'difficulty in establishing the full extent of its liabilities'. A civil servant, however competent, is unlikely to have the experience needed to run a large-scale public attraction, and the fact that her replacement was recruited from Eurodisney suggests that this was recognized, but too late to overcome all the problems.

The importance of purpose, structure and managerial competence

This example of the Millennium Dome has shown that the three-legged stool view of an organization works even for the most complex examples. The problems faced by Equitable Life and Marconi in the UK, and Enron, WorldCom and Global Crossing in the USA at the beginning of the twenty-first century have certainly proved this to be the case. Failure can stare any organization in the face if it does not:

- define a clear purpose;
- establish a structure appropriate to achieving that purpose;
- manage at every level to gain continuing commitment from the vast majority of staff for most of the time.

Communication is at the heart of the third leg of the stool and is fundamental to managerial competence at all levels. A manager's job is to get things done through other people, however large the organization may be.

4 Types of organization

Many types of organization have developed over the centuries, ranging from the sole trader, through partnerships in which a number of people pool their resources and expertise, to private or public limited companies, with tens or thousands of shareholders. There are also organizations, such as co-operative societies and trades unions, which have evolved to give their members collective strength to counterbalance that of organizations with whom they must negotiate or compete. And there are charities, some of them very large organizations employing many paid staff as well as volunteers.

We have looked at the different requirements made on organizations by different purposes and the way in which their structure needs to reflect their purpose. Many legal requirements are placed on organizations too, as you will see in this section.

4.1 The sole trader

Sole traders, in particular, are responsible for many inventions and innovations. If you work for an oil refining company and design a new form of engine which doesn't use petrol, you may not be too popular – think of all the 'vested interest' they have in petrol refining, amounting to billions of pounds. But, as an individual, you might be able to sell such an idea to a large company which does not have an interest in suppressing it.

The vast majority of businesses in the UK are small, with more than 80% employing fewer than ten people. A large proportion of these are in the sole trader category.

This is the simplest form of business to run, from an organizational and internal communications point of view, as it is typically a self-employed person. Motivation is provided automatically for most by the basic need to earn a living in the absence of a regular wage or salary.

However, there are many pressures on the sole trader, whatever trade or profession is being pursued.

Activity 4 · 3 mins

From your own experience, list some examples of 'sole traders' with whom you have dealt:

■ in trades, such as shopkeepers or window cleaning;
■ in professions, such as dentistry or general practice as a doctor.

_____

_____

_____

_____

■ List any pressures you think any sole trader might be under, in what you consider to be the order of significance.

_____

_____

_____

The examples of sole traders are so many and various that your list could contain any number of examples, from fishmongers to soul singers and shoe-makers to authors.

As far as the pressures go, these are common to all of them. You have probably listed many of the following, even if you haven't put them in the same order.

- Staying healthy – illness is a constant anxiety for anyone 'going it alone'.
- Deciding what business is 'right for you'.
- Getting business from credit worthy customers.
- Meeting the quality standards of customers.
- Getting paid in reasonable time.
- Providing money for working capital, capital investment and the future.
- Accounting for the monies received and paid.
- Keeping up to date with the law and their own speciality.
- Using time effectively.

The list of broad categories shows that the sole trader has to look after most of the functions which the largest 'mega corporation' has. He or she must also do it without the help of specialist managers found in large organizations unless, of course, they:

- buy services in from accountants, lawyers, marketing or other specialists;
- join a trade association or federation that can provide them with back-up services as part of the membership package, for which they pay an annual fee.

The sole trader does not have to manage internal human resources, but must:

- deal effectively with people who are customers, suppliers and employees of official bodies;
- if wise, practise rigorous 'self appraisal' on every aspect of personal performance.

Most attention in the media is focused on the very largest organizations in the public and private sectors. However, much of the dynamism and original thinking that a country needs are generated by sole traders and small businesses. They are free of the shackles of vested interests, hierarchies and rigid reporting relationships, all of which often smother new ideas in large organizations.

The government and other organizations are increasingly recognizing the importance of small organizations to the UK.

The Confederation of British Industry (CBI), though associated in most people's minds with 'big business', has an Enterprise Group devoted to furthering the interests of smaller businesses. It acts both to influence the UK government and the European Union (EU).

In 2002, the Labour government stated that it wished to become the party of the small business and the self-employed as well as of employees.

Unlimited liability

Undoubtedly, the threat to a sole trader's personal assets is one of the greatest sources of anxiety. The law provides protection for the shareholders of incorporated private and public companies through limited liability (which we will discuss in section 4.3). However, the law does not allow a sole trader to register as a limited liability company. And even if it did, many businesses would undoubtedly demand personal guarantees, secured on the trader's private property – typically a house – before agreeing to give them medium- or long-term credit in the form of, for example, bank loans or overdrafts.

If large customers are slow to pay, or don't pay at all through insolvency or fraud, then the sole trader can be placed in a desperate financial position. Lloyds members (see the margin box) are not alone in facing financial disaster. Many a sole trader, in sport, entertainment, commerce and industry, has lost everything after a seemingly glittering career. Often, it is through unwise speculation, poor financial management – or the attentions of 'fair-weather friends' who melted away at the first signs of chill winds blowing away the fortune that they had been helping to 'manage'.

Until limited liability companies were recognized by the law (in the mid-nineteenth century), the threat to individuals' personal assets was a real barrier to enterprise. The threat was there for both sole traders and partners in an unincorporated partnership.

> The consequences of unlimited liability are shown by what happened to many 'names' in the Lloyds Insurance business, following several years of disasters in the 1990s. Many of the largest risks were insured by Lloyds and they called upon the 'names' or members to pay. At the time, it was a condition that the names accepted unlimited personal liability. Many lost virtually everything they possessed, amounting to hundreds of thousands of pounds or more

4.2 Partnerships

There are many practical advantages to taking the step from being a sole trader to becoming a member of a partnership.

Activity 5

3 mins

What advantages should a partnership business have over that of a sole trader? Jot down at least four.

_____

_____

_____

Your list of advantages could have included:

- having more capital available to invest without borrowing and paying interest to a bank or other third party;
- having a wider range of skills and contacts available;
- avoiding the need to employ expensive specialists (e.g. in accountancy, information technology, marketing) to do jobs which various partners can undertake;
- having more chance to manage time effectively and spread the administrative burden involved in running any business;
- having opportunities to discuss and resolve immediate problems, including competitors' activities, with a sympathetic group of people;
- having the chance to generate new ideas through discussions and brainstorming sessions;
- having the facility to review performance in every aspect of the business and look for continuous improvement;
- having someone to take over if a key partner is away on holiday, ill, or in any other way unable to give the business their full attention for an extended period of time.

Surely the main advantage is that you no longer have to be a 'one-person band'.

Each can focus on what they are good at if, say:

- one partner can produce wonderful ideas which work, but is naturally shy;
- another is an extrovert who loves dealing with customers;
- and another understands financial matters.

Of course, they still need to agree on the three broad issues:

- What the organization is setting out to do.
- What structure will be used to ensure effort is not duplicated and what responsibility and authority each partner has.
- How the business will be managed at each level, to ensure that everyone – including employees who are not partners – remain committed to its purpose.

Equal or unequal partners?

Members of partnerships are often equal partners, sharing the risks, responsibilities and rewards equally. However, the partnership deed, under which the partnership is registered legally can apportion all of these matters in any way that the partners agree upon. Some may take a much more active role than others and be rewarded accordingly.

There may be 'sleeping partners', who provide capital and share in any profits made, but take no active part in the day-to-day running of the business.

In *Animal Farm*, George Orwell's 1940s allegorical tale on the move to the totalitarian organization of society, the pigs gain the upper hand. They declare that 'all the animals are equal, but some are more equal than others' – a mathematical impossibility but a reality in many societies – and partnerships.

Many partnerships are relatively small, close-knit operations – often in professions such as the law, accountancy, or property services operating locally. But you may have come across some which have many, even hundreds, of partners, such as some of the national and international partnerships in law, property, accountancy and management consultancy.

In practice, the very large firms have moved right away from the original idea of a few people sharing their expertise and financial resources. They must operate just like any other large organization.

Some of the partners are 'more equal than the others'.

Can you imagine a committee of hundreds of equal partners reaching a decision about anything in a reasonable time?

Disadvantages of partnerships

One disadvantage that all partners share with sole traders is that of unlimited liability. This can be a real disincentive to borrowing money from outside the partnership. But it is not the only, or indeed the chief, reason why so many partnerships fail and often end up in acrimonious court proceedings.

Activity 6 · 2 mins

Can you suggest three or four factors that may undermine partnerships which, if not addressed, can lead them to be dissolved?

_____

_____

_____

A whole series of TV programmes has focused on the stresses that arise when groups of individuals are put together in demanding situations with no defined leader. At its worst, a partnership may exhibit the same destructive tendencies.

You probably listed factors, including the jealousies and clashes of personality that beset any group of equals working under pressure. 'I do all the work, but they're getting as much as I am' is a common complaint. Simple dishonesty, where one partner absconds with partnership funds, or employs 'friends' at inflated prices to act as sub-contractors, is another. Spouses, relatives and friends may be given partnership roles on the basis of friendship rather than business acumen or saleable skills.

The business may grow beyond the level at which some partners are competent to manage – but the agreement may still provide that partner with a right to take decisions that the others cannot challenge.

Succession can be a real problem if a partner retires, decides to pursue another career or has an accident. The partnership really exists only as the sum of the skills and experience that individual partners bring to it. Its effectiveness can quickly decline if one or more of the key people leave, or become less effective, for any reason.

Of course, many partnerships survive for decades or longer, well beyond the working lives of the original partners. This is because they have found a way of organizing their affairs to ensure that the 'three-legged stool' remains stable, that is:

- they continue to have a clear purpose, adapted to suit changes in the requirements of customers and clients;
- their organizational structure is well-defined;
- the partners who manage the entity are competent leaders, who communicate effectively and continue to motivate their fellow partners and employees.

Partnerships really can have advantages over the sole trader. It is significant that they so often involve people in professions that do not need to raise large amounts of finance for premises or capital equipment.

4.3 Limited companies

In the USA the letters 'Inc.' stand for 'incorporated body', and in France 'SA' stands for 'Société Anonyme'. Both signify organizations that are distinct legal entities which have limited liability.

Together with the public sector corporations, limited liability companies are the largest organizations in the UK economy. There are equivalent organizations in every developed country, with a similar legal status and operating in similar fashion. Because people hold individual shares, or 'bundles' of shares called stocks, such companies are often referred to as 'joint stock' companies.

So, what is the significance of the 'Ltd' abbreviation, or the letters 'plc' after the name of a large organization like Boots, Halifax, or Corus? In law, it is a very significant one. Any company incorporated under the Companies Act and registered by the Registrar of Companies at Companies House is regarded as having a distinct personality. The incorporated company assumes an identity legally separate from that of the directors and managers who run it.

The limited company can:

- make contracts, or be sued, in its own name;
- be prosecuted under the criminal laws and Acts of Parliament, such as the Health and Safety at Work Act;
- has liability limited to the value of its issued share capital.

The South Sea Bubble occurred when the English South Sea Company sold so many shares that it volunteered to finance the English national debt. There was a 900% rise in the price of the shares, but the Bubble burst in 1720 and the value of the shares plummeted. Thousands of investors were bankrupted, driving some into exile or even to suicide.

After the scandal of the 'South Sea Bubble' in the early eighteenth century, successive British governments were wary of allowing the formation of any joint stock companies, seeing them as providing opportunities for wholesale fraud and deception. However, as the industrial revolution proceeded, private individuals found it difficult to raise large sums of capital. They were unwilling to risk their entire fortunes in sole trader enterprises. Eventually, the joint stock company was rehabilitated, by a series of Acts of Parliament that began in 1844.

There have since been so many Acts and amendments, and the Law is now so complicated, that many lawyers do nothing but work in this area. Numerous textbooks are devoted to the topic. Here we will focus on the broad principles, particularly:

The difference between a Private Limited Company and a Public Limited Company (plc) is that the former is not allowed to offer its shares for sale to the general public.

- the consequences of limited liability;
- the ability of limited liability companies to raise large sums of capital;
- the way in which an organization with a 'fictitious personality' must be managed.

Limited liability

This protection for the shareholders of a company grants them great peace of mind. In essence, the law says that there can be no greater demand made upon shareholders than the value of the shares they have agreed to buy.

Activity 7

2 mins

Michael agreed to subscribe to a share offer made by a limited company. He bought 1,000 shares in a company for £7.50 per share. He was to pay £2.50 per share initially, and two further instalments of £2.50 when 'called' for by the company. He paid the second instalment, or 'call', after 18 months. Three months later, the company went into liquidation and his shares became effectively worthless.

- The company's debts amounted to £10,000,000.
- There were 1,000 shareholders.
- So the average 'debt per shareholder' was £10,000,000/1,000 = £10,000.

What was Michael's actual maximum liability for the company's debts?

Under the law, Michael was only liable to pay the balance remaining on the shares he had agreed to buy – that is, £2,500. This represented just one quarter of the amount that averaging the company's debts over the total number of shareholders would produce. Of course, he had also lost £5,000 through paying the first two calls. But contrast his situation with that of the unhappy Lloyds' names referred to earlier.

Protection for creditors and 'third parties' generally

Much of company law is aimed at protecting those who deal with limited companies, including their employees, from dishonest company managers. This can give an observer a negative view of limited liability companies, not improved by the accounting scandals of their US counterparts in the early twenty-first century.

However, in practice the vast majority of companies run their affairs honestly and it is generally thought that accounting standards required in the UK are significantly higher than those in the USA. The advantages to the total UK economy of raising capital for large-scale businesses, which would otherwise not exist, far outweigh the disadvantages and problems caused by a small number of unscrupulous operators.

In some circumstances, the courts can 'lift the veil' of incorporation, in the graphic phrase used by the lawyers. Where there is evidence of wrongdoing, such as trading while the directors know a company does not have enough money to cover its liabilities, the courts can proceed directly against the assets of company directors who have acted in ways that prejudice the interests of third parties.

Raising capital

Whereas a private limited company has a legal upper limit placed on the number of its shareholders and cannot sell shares to the general public, the public limited company (plc) has no such limitations. It can therefore raise large amounts of capital both from individuals and from other companies.

If you think about a business venture requiring £25 million to establish itself, the arithmetic shows clearly how powerful an organization the 'plc' is for raising capital.

- A sole trader would have to use his or her own resources, or borrow from banks on the security of their own fortune. Few people would be able *and* willing to raise £25 million in this way.
- A partnership is in a better position, but if there were 25 partners, they would need to raise £1 million each and would still have 'unlimited liability'.
- A private limited company with 50 shareholders, would have to demand an average of £0.5 million from each of them (though at least their liability would be limited).
- *But* a 'plc' could sell shares to any number of investors. If sold to 10,000 people, their average liability would be limited to £2,500 – a much more reasonable sum.

This example explains clearly why the 'plc' is able to raise such enormous sums fairly simply, subject to many legal safeguards as to what the company is allowed to do with the money. It explains why virtually all the largest companies in the UK are 'plc's, though there are some very large private limited companies, usually still mainly under the control of the family which founded the business.

Managing an organization with a separate legal identity

Though an incorporated company has its own legal personality, it cannot actually do anything without human intervention. That, coupled with limited liability, has caused the law to prescribe:

- that a company may only legally do what the 'memorandum of association' (filed prior to registration) sets out as its purpose;
- how, in general terms, the company must manage its affairs, as set out in its 'Articles of Association' (also part of the registration process).

The memorandum of association

The Rover company originally made bicycles, towards the end of the nineteenth century. If its memorandum of association had stated that the sole purpose of the company was to manufacture and sell bicycles, it would have been unable to diversify into motor cars some years later, unless it went through a tedious legal process.

Think back to the 'three-legged stool' for a moment. In essence, the memorandum sets out the *purpose* of the company that forms its first leg. It cannot do anything else without going through a legal process to amend its memorandum. This is completely different from a sole trader or partnership, which can choose to do anything it wishes to, at any time – provided of course that it is itself legal.

This provision can be very limiting on a plc's activities. Though it is often obvious what a company intends to do to earn a living, it is not always so. And companies often need to change over the years, as the markets that they serve change.

Company directors now draw up their memoranda in very broad terms, enabling them to change and diversify without the need for amendment.

Activity 8 · 2 mins

Suggest how the memorandum of association could be worded to allow the Rover Company to diversify from manufacturing bicycles to manufacturing motor cars, filling in the gaps in this sentence.

'The purpose of this Company is to manufacture, distribute and sell _____ form of _____ for use by individuals or public service operators.'

You will find a suggestion in the Answers to activities on page 206. It may differ from your own, but the basic point is that by saying they were in the transport business, or words to that effect, the company gives itself room to manufacture anything from a pogo stick to a motor coach, an aircraft or an ocean liner.

Many companies developed into conglomerates in the twentieth century, involving themselves in an extremely wide range of activities.

There are fashions in business, as well as on the catwalk. Conglomerates are now out of fashion and Tomkins has sold many of its businesses – including both the 'guns and buns' makers.

> The multi-billion-pound turnover Tomkins plc company became known as the 'guns to buns' company in the City of London, during the 1990s because it ran businesses that included gun manufacture (in the USA) lawnmowers, plumbing supplies, rubber components for cars and aircraft, windscreen wiper blades, birthday cakes (for Marks & Spencer) gravy browning, bread, frozen meat pies – and yes, buns.
>
> You would never have guessed this from the simple name Tomkins. On the other hand, it's apparent that the former British Steel Corporation (now part of Corus) was likely to be involved in steel making.

The articles of association

Copies of both the memorandum and articles of association are public documents, which anyone can inspect through Companies House. It's worth doing if you have any concerns about dealing with a company, to assure yourself about exactly what the company is able to do legally.

These, for a limited company, provide the second leg of the stool, setting out its permanent organizational structure. The articles specify:

- how directors are to be appointed and what authority they have;
- how powers are to be allocated between the directors and the shareholders.

These articles cannot be changed without the agreement of shareholders, another safeguard for investors.

The 'directing mind'

Despite these legal safeguards, it can still be difficult to know who is really responsible for a company's actions. The larger the organization, the farther is the 'man or woman at the top' from its activities at grass-roots level.

Many vast organizations are clearly identified with a particular person. Bill Gates, the founder of Microsoft – one of the world's largest organizations   is clearly identified with it. Richard Branson is likewise identified with Virgin and all the businesses it operates.

If you think back to the sole trader, there is no problem in deciding who made a decision over any aspect of the business. But when it comes to a huge plc employing tens of thousands, at hundreds of sites, every second of the year, it becomes a very different matter.

What the law tries to do, however vast an organization may be, is identify a senior figure as the 'directing mind'. This person can be held accountable for an event, wherever and whenever it happened. It may involve finance, safety, product quality, environmental health – indeed anything that concerns those who deal with an organization or work for it. Even in the largest company, there must be someone who is ultimately responsible, just as there is in the very smallest 'sole trader' business.

4.4 Public sector, voluntary sector and 'self help' organizations

So far in this book we have dealt chiefly with organizations in the private sector, which usually have to make a profit to survive. However, there is an enormous public sector which provides many essential services to the community.

Activity 9

3 mins

List up to six organizations that operate in the public sector, either by type or by quoting specific examples in your own area.

_____

_____

_____

What do you think is one **major** difference between private companies and public sector organizations?

_____

_____

You will find a list of organizations that operate in the public sector in the Answers to activities on page 206.

Profit centre vs Cost centre

The major difference between private companies and public sector organizations is that, broadly speaking, private organizations are **profit** centres. They must make a profit to survive, whereas public sector bodies are **cost** centres, which must aim to control their spending within allocated budgets. They do not usually have to make a surplus, or profit, to fund new investment.

Nevertheless, the three-legged stool model applies just as well to public sector organizations as to any other. They must:

■ be clear what their purpose is;
■ have an appropriate organizational structure;
■ manage their employees at all levels to retain their commitment.

Public sector organizations are answerable to local or central government and through them to the electorate. The electors have the ultimate say as to whether their objectives are the right ones and whether they are being achieved at an acceptable cost.

The voluntary sector

Charities including the RSPCA and its Scottish equivalent, the NSPCC, Barnardo's, Oxfam, the Cheshire Homes and St. John's Ambulance, control substantial funds. Much of their income is in the form of legacies that the donor entrusts them with after his or her death.

Private charity is an honourable and long-established aspect of British life. Visit any town or city and you will probably find almshouses, often endowed by benefactors hundreds of years ago, but still carrying out the original purpose of their founders. Since these founders are long dead, they must have established a structure, in the form of a charitable trust, to ensure that their intentions would continue to be carried out. There are many larger charities whose names are household words, again many of them long-established and still basically doing what their founders intended them to do.

A formal legal process must be followed to establish a charity. The body set up to vet and oversee their establishment and subsequent activities is the Charity Commission, which is approximately equivalent to the Registrar of Companies.

The purpose of a charity

As with a limited company, the purpose must be clearly stated in the registration document and in practice, will be more narrowly focused than that of most limited companies. It would be difficult or impossible to register a charity with very far-reaching aims.

Imagine a charity that supported vivisection for medical research on the one hand and opposed all cruelty to animals on the other. These are mutually incompatible and there would probably be very few donors to the charity.

Activity 10 · 2 mins

A charity was registered with the object of 'improving the lot of working horses in the Indian sub continent'. Some years later, a request was received from a field worker in India for funds to mitigate the plight of mules and donkeys working in an industrial brickfield near New Delhi.

- Could the charity legally help? YES/NO
- If not, what would it need to do so that it could?

_____

_____

_____

The charity would have been unable to help as things stood legally. Although donkeys and mules are related species, they are *not* horses and its objective was helping horses. It would need to amend its purpose, with the consent of its supporters, to read more generally. If it substituted the word 'equines' for horses, then horses, donkeys, zebras and any other equine species could be helped legally.

Because charities are entrusted with large sums of money, often in cash, the rules governing how they must operate and what they are allowed to do with the money have to be very strict. Charities do enormous good with the money they receive in the UK and throughout the world.

Charities *have* to be above suspicion, or their funding will reduce and they will be much less able to serve the causes they were established to help.

In the case of all the organizations described, there are specific legal requirements as to registration and the ways in which they must be run to retain their status and legal recognition.

Other organizations with roots in charity and 'self help'

In this session we've looked at several important types of organization, but there are still many more.

Activity 11

2 mins

What types of organization have not yet been described in this session but are important in UK Society? List three or four significant ones.

_____

_____

_____

You may well have suggested any of the items in the list given in the Answers to activities on page 206. Those which continue to have a significant effect on the UK's economy and social fabric are described below.

■ **Trades unions**
Workers began to organize themselves to counterbalance the power of their employers. Though the focus of unions has changed, they remain important organizations, which depend on a great deal of voluntary work at the shop (or office) floor level. They provide a wide range of welfare services to members as well as negotiating payment and conditions of work with their employers. They have also been heavily involved with Health and Safety legislation, which has helped improve the conditions of work for everyone.

- **Co-operative societies**

  Co-operative societies are immensely important commercially, and collectively they figure amongst the UK's largest retailing organizations. They retain close affinity to their roots in the industrial towns of the nineteenth century and take a strong ethical stance over many issues concerning the UK and countries in the developing world. Some directors may be elected to the board from amongst employees and society members. There is a strong emphasis on supporting local communities.

- **Building societies**

  Many have now changed their status and become plcs. However, there are a significant number of societies registered under specific building societies legislation, which allows them less commercial freedom. They contend that they can offer a better and more economical service to their members by retaining their original status.

- **Mutual and friendly societies**

  These organizations were closely related to insurance companies. They provided very inexpensive policies to help poorer people to 'help themselves', particularly against sickness, old age and funeral expenses. Many of their functions have now been taken over by the state, or are provided for in other ways. Originally, they demonstrated yet another way in which people could organize themselves, even in adverse circumstances, and produce a result whose sum was 'greater than the sum of its parts'.

We've seen that the many ways in which people can organize themselves are reflected in the different types of organization. They are also reflected in the range of structures that organizations adopt, a subject to which we turn in the next section.

'Form should follow function' is a well-recognized principle of architecture. It stands to reason that a castle should have a different structure from a hotel, a school from a prison and a domestic house from a hotel.

5 Organizational structures

'Structure' includes the allocation of formal responsibilities, the typical organization chart. It also covers the linking mechanisms between the roles ...'

Charles Handy, *Understanding Organizations*

Charts are a very useful means to describe organizations. They will be used in this section to help explore the strengths and weaknesses of different types.

5.1 Hierarchical structures

Roles within a hierarchy

Organizations are often shown as a triangle.

- The Managing Director or Chief Executive at the apex at the top.
- Then a board of directors, each taking responsibility for a defined function, such as Finance.
- At the next level, departmental managers who report to the functional director: in Finance, these might comprise information technology, accounting, payroll, data protection.
- Then first line managers who report to each departmental manager: in accounting they might look after accounts payable, accounts receivable, credit control and bank transactions.
- Finally, at the base, the operators who do the routine work, which would be clerical staff in the case of the Finance Department.

Responsibilities at different levels

The job titles and number of layers will vary with the size and type of organization. But there are factors that all hierarchies have in common.

- In general terms, the closer a manager is to the apex of the triangle, the less he or she should be involved with day-to-day routine. The Managing Director should be concerned predominately with long-term strategy, with looking at external influences on the organization; with judging its strengths, its weaknesses, the opportunities which it should grasp and the threats it must counter.
- The nearer to the base that a manager operates, the more he or she must be concerned with ensuring that the daily routines of selling, manufacturing, distributing and accounting for earned and spent money operate efficiently.
- The roles are mutually dependent – there's no point having a marvellous strategic thinker as Managing Director if the business is haemorrhaging money on a daily basis. Conversely, first line managers will be wasting their time and energies controlling day-to-day affairs if the company is heading in the wrong direction for the medium or long term.
- The nearer to the apex you get, the less obvious it becomes what you *should* be doing.

Many senior managers find it very hard to think about the long term and immerse themselves in the detail of day-to-day activity because they wish to be busy and earn their salaries. Nearer to the base level, managers and staff can become disillusioned and disaffected if there is constant interference, or if the organization's purpose is not clear to them and they are unsure about just what they are meant to be doing.

Why have so many layers and functions?

Reverting to the sole trader for a moment, role and responsibility are clear-cut and there is no complex structure to get in the way. All the functions are in the trader's own hands. But large organizations need to have defined responsibilities and lines of communication if they are to run smoothly: there isn't time for one manager to look after several complicated functions. It's also impossible for everyone to talk to everyone else, or for decisions to be made by committees involving everyone in an organization that employs hundreds or thousands of people.

A typical hierarchy

The diagram below shows a typical hierarchical structure for a large organization, with several tiers of management between the most senior and least senior members. If the structure is adhered to rigidly, then there will be no contact directly between the different 'lines', such as F-E-D-C-B-A and F-G-H-I-J-K.

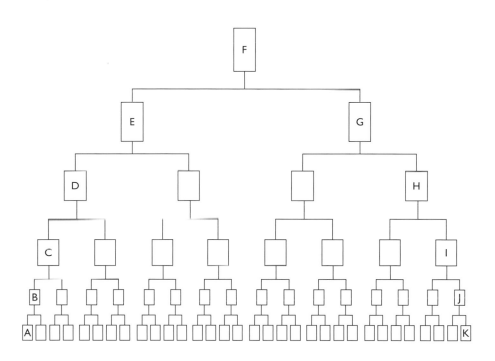

Such structures have been traditional in the armed services, the police, in large engineering companies and effectively in multi-site operations – retailing, catering and distribution. Each of the blocks across from level C might represent a local depot manager with two supervisors reporting to him.

Activity 12

What do you think are:

- the advantages of such a structure;
- the disadvantages?

Relate your answers to your own experiences, with present or previous employers and with other organizations you have dealt with.

_____

_____

_____

_____

Advantages of hierarchical structures could include the following.

- Everyone knows where they stand, who reports to them and to whom they report. If the structure is implemented logically, people at every level will know exactly what the limits of their authority are.
- There is an identifiable promotional path from level A to level F, though there are obviously many fewer jobs at the higher levels.
- In the military sphere, if someone is killed or incapacitated in battle, succession is automatic on the basis of rank (and seniority, for example, if the brigadier at level D is killed and there are two colonels at Level C in the diagram, then the Colonel who had been promoted to that rank first would take over).

The disadvantages could include the following.

- The rigidity of the structure can encourage lack of initiative and a 'jobsworth' attitude.
- Communication can be very slow between the different 'lines'. For example, what happens if the manager at any level is away?
- Where quick reactions are required 'on the ground', the people best able to take the decision may be forbidden to do so until the message has gone up to level F and come all the way back down again. By that time, it may be too late.

In practice, relationships between people in different lines will almost always develop for any number of reasons. If, for example, your brother or someone you were at school with, works in another department, will you really never use that link to 'get things done' outside the formal structure? Or if you are a local manager with initiative and integrity, will you always wait for a remote senior manager to tell you how to do your job?

> A young management services manager was assigned to a project in Nigeria, where her organization had a depot in Lagos. On the third day of her project, the local General Manager, George Deauville, said 'Oh, by the way, Nicky, I've arranged for us to go up to Ibadan to look at the depot there this weekend.'
>
> 'How long have we had a depot there? They didn't mention it to me back in London,' replied Nicky, puzzled.
>
> 'That's because I haven't told them yet,' replied Deauville. 'I was sure there was a good opportunity there – it's one of the largest cities in Africa.'
>
> 'But what happens if it fails?' persisted Nicky.
>
> 'It won't. But, if it should, then I'll close it or sell it – and no one at Head Office will be any the wiser, unless you tell them. Would you?'
>
> Nicky smiled and shook her head.

This true story shows that people 'on the spot' with initiative, local knowledge and spirit will usually find ways of overcoming the more restrictive aspects of a hierarchy, even if they aren't several thousand miles away from 'head office'.

5.2 The 'wheel'

The next diagram is of another structure with which you may be familiar. It shows ten team members revolving around one designated chief decision maker. All the team members really are equal and all may talk to each other if they wish to.

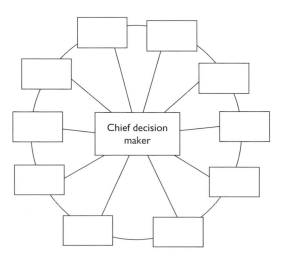

Activity 13 · 4 mins

Again, referring to your own experiences where possible, note down what you believe to be:

■ the advantages of this management structure;
■ its disadvantages.

_____

_____

_____

_____

_____

_____

_____

The founders of Tesco, Marks and Spencer and the Burton tailoring group all remained at the hub of their businesses for many years after they had become substantial businesses, far removed from their basic origins as small-scale retailers and tailors.

The fact that everyone is able to talk to each other has some advantages. But it can also have drawbacks in that, since nobody but the person at the centre of the wheel can take decisions, the other ten people may become little more than a 'talking shop'.

The decision maker, of course, should know very quickly what is going on and be able to respond swiftly to changing circumstances. But, what happens if he or she is away for any reason? Or lacks the expertise and insight to weigh up the situation correctly and so makes a wrong decision?

Though this structure is typical of smaller companies, it is not that uncommon to find large organizations, even governments, that revolve entirely around one central decision taker, most often to their detriment.

The transition from a 'small' business, where such a structure can be successful, to a larger one that is usually beyond the capacity of one person to keep a grasp on, is one of the most difficult to make. Many fall by the wayside, or sell out to larger organizations that have the organizational expertise to cope with the complexities and sheer volumes of data generated by large-scale activity in the public, private or voluntary sectors.

5.3 Flat management structure

Many companies have tried to delayer their hierarchies and remove tiers of management – and cost – in the process. A structure that has been subject to this approach is shown in this diagram.

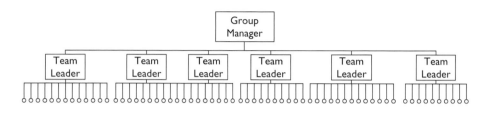

Activity 14 · 3 mins

■ What conditions do you think must be met if a 'flat' management structure is to work successfully?

_____

_____

■ For what overall *purposes* might it be the ideal choice?

_____

_____

The designated team leaders must have sufficient delegated authority for such an organization to work. They must also have the expertise and self-confidence to run their affairs without constant reference to their 'boss' for guidance and support.

Organizations that are bad at delegating authority will struggle if this structure is imposed, and the team leader's authority and self confidence will be constantly undermined.

Opportunities for promotion are likely to be few in a 'delayered' hierarchy, which can demotivate ambitious people.

A flat organization is ideally suited to the purpose of growing a number of 'sub-organizations' quickly in parallel. A charity, for example, that wishes to expand rapidly, might do so, using dedicated people in the team leader role. They may be volunteers with no wish for promotion.

If you have worked for an organization which has stripped away layers of management, you will have your own experience and opinions as to its advantages and potential pitfalls.

5.4 Functional management structure

The three forms of organizational structure that we've looked at so far have something in common: they provide a designated leader at some point. But is this always necessary?

The functional management structure says there doesn't have to be one leader.

The next diagram shows such a structure, under which the line managers report separately to whichever function is involved with their current activity. For a new product launch, that might be the group marketing manager; for a new engineering project it might be the group engineering controller and so on. The site may or may not have a designated 'general manager'.

FUNCTIONAL MANAGEMENT STRUCTURE

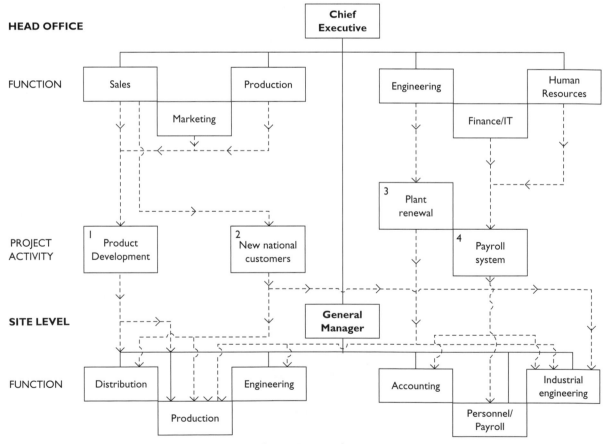

Note: Chart shows situation when four projects are happening together, a normal situation for a large organization to be in

Activity 15

3 mins

■ This is a quite different approach to structuring organizations. Like the others we have looked at, it has its strengths and weaknesses. What do you think they are?

_____

_____

_____

■ Can you suggest an overall organizational purpose that it is well suited to?

_____

_____

_____

The advantages to the line manager may be that he or she has constant access to genuine expertise and to senior managers able to provide support.

Against that, the line manager can suffer the classic dilemma of serving two (if not several) masters, some of whose demands are conflicting, all of whom are senior in rank and between whom he or she cannot arbitrate. In addition, they have no responsibility for general site issues, such as employee relations, security, health, safety, cleaning, general maintenance and relationships with the local community.

The site manager, if there is one, loses much authority to people beyond his or her control and yet retains responsibility for anything that is done which may prejudice the general standards of management. If there is _no_ site manager, then who takes responsibility for all the general matters?

Like the other structures, the functional structure has a place, possibly in an organization directed towards marketing or design-led activities.

5.5 What are the objects of organizational structures?

In the descriptions of organizational structures, words like 'up'; 'down'; 'more senior' and so on are used, implying that some staff are 'more equal than others'. That is evidently true, in terms of the rewards which people tend to receive as they progress 'up' through an organization. But:

■ should a management structure be built upon the shoulders of the people who drive the buses, staff the charity shops, teach the children, deliver the mail – in fact do any of the countless jobs usually shown at the bottom of the chart?

■ or should the structure exist to underpin their activities, requiring managers to bear those for whom they take responsibility upon *their* shoulders?

Particularly if you have been promoted from the shop floor, you will probably have your own views on this.

> The BBC ran a series of TV programmes called 'Back to the floor' in which senior managers, in widely differing businesses, worked alongside their shop floor colleagues. Though they did not do so 'incognito', their common experience was that too often their people and the FLMs (first line managers) who managed them were *imposed upon*, rather than *supported by* the organizations for whom they worked.

A major manufacturing group faced a national strike. Management and supervisory staff were not involved and nor were some shop floor employees. Many sites were able to carry on limited production.

It was immediately apparent that the key activity was packaging, involving fearsomely complicated machines, many of which appeared to have 'minds of their own'. An impromptu management structure was soon evolved in which it was recognized that the key 'managers' were:

■ experienced supervisors, engineers and operatives who understood these machines and could operate and maintain them.

The more senior managers' role became one of supporting their junior colleagues by:

■ ensuring that supplies of raw materials and packaging continued to arrive in the right amounts;

■ servicing the packaging machine operators by physically moving the stocks of finished products and packaging materials to them.

Much of the work that senior managers did would have been considered unskilled labour, and they took instruction from the junior colleagues who were much 'closer to the action' than they were.

This example is not intended to demean the role of senior managers under normal circumstances, when they should properly be concerned with medium to longer-term issues. It simply underlines that:

■ structures need to be designed to suit the purpose that the organization is seeking to achieve, in this case keeping the business going;
■ the aim of management should be to reduce the burden on those who do the work that earns the organization its living;
■ it is no bad thing for managers at every level to find out just how much they depend on the people who are so often spoken of in the media as being at the shop floor level.

5.6 Reorganization

Writing around AD 60, Petronius Arbiter said: 'I was to learn later in life that we tend to meet any new situation by reorganizing. What a wonderful method it can be for creating the illusion of progress whilst producing confusion, inefficiency and demoralization.'

Depending on whom you have worked for, you will have experienced reorganization more or less frequently. The quotation from Petronius Arbiter is close to 2,000 years old, but may well raise a wry smile from you.

Many organizations in the public, private and voluntary sectors seem to reorganize with astounding frequency, often producing confusion, inefficiency and demoralization.

Even seemingly 'minor' changes, like moving the number of accounting periods in a year from calendar months to 13 '4-week periods' can cause confusion. The ability to compare like with like disappears and managers waste time reconciling figures and arguing about whether this year is really worse, or better, than last.

More major changes, like changes from a hierarchical or wheel structure, can have effects which last for years. In the worst cases, they can divert attention from the real purpose of the organization, whether it be public service, charitable or making continuing profits to assure the survival of the business. Large organizations frequently carry special provisions on their annual accounts for the costs of reorganization (or restructuring).

In principle, *evolution* is better than *revolution* when it comes to changing organizational structures.

All senior managers would do well to keep in mind the accounting maxim that 'no profits are generated *inside* a business, only costs.'

Though voluntary and public sector organizations are normally cost centres, rather than profit centres, they are still subject to this same financial 'law'.

■ The more they spend on internal matters, including reorganization, the harder it will be to manage within their budget ...
■ and the less will be available for public service or charitable works.

6 Organizational functions

We've considered the difficulty that a sole trader has in being 'all things to all persons'. In larger organizations, the problem is overcome by employing specialists in various fields. The result is the typical organization chart shown here.

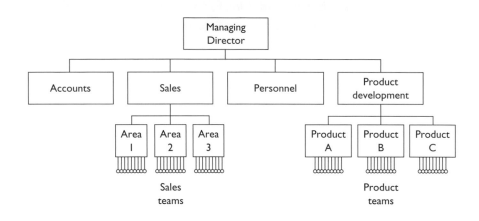

The context within which all organizations must work is now so complex that it would be impossible for the larger ones to survive without access to specialists.

- Employment law alone can be a 'minefield' for organizations in the public, private and voluntary sectors. Thousands, or even millions of £s can be at stake if sound policies do not exist, or are not implemented.
- Inexpert management of building and construction projects can bankrupt even a large company, or result in it being prosecuted by the Health and Safety Executive or the Environment Agency for breaches of the law.

Though specialist managers bring many benefits to an organization, they can also create problems of their own.

Activity 16

List up to ten specialist functions that a medium- to large-scale organization needs to run effectively.

_____

_____

_____

_____

■ What might be the problems of integrating them?

_____

_____

■ How, in principle, do you think these problems might be overcome?

_____

_____

You will find a suggested range of functions in the Answers to activities on page 206.

The heads of specialist functions will take a professional pride in their expertise and could be thought of as similar to the 'stars' in a sports team, or the principals in an orchestra.

Each will probably 'fight their corner', believing the discipline they represent to be the most important to the organization's well being. Up to a point, that is healthy, but it can lead to problems if all or some of them pull in different directions.

In principle, it is for the organization's general manager, managing director, chief executive (however the office is designated) to:

■ instil in the specialists respect for its overall *purpose*;
■ provide a structure that gives recognition to their expertise;
■ manage and communicate with them to maintain their commitment to the purpose;

■ ensure that, overall, the total of their contributions is greater than the sum of its parts.

This last point must be the objective of organizations in every sphere of human activity; otherwise there is no point in having them.

■ Achieve this objective and the organization will be effective – but virtually invisible.

Self-assessment 1

20 mins

1 Complete this sentence.

The sign of a _____ organization is that the _____ is _____ than the sum of its parts.

2 Which of the following is the basis for continuing success in any successful organization in the long term? Underline your choice.

power/success/sound financial management/
excellent management communications/marketing

3 Put a tick against the correct answer.

Investing in a company's shares removes from investors the threat of

■ business failure;
■ unlimited personal liability;
■ take over by a larger business;
■ poor management decisions.

4 Suggest two disadvantages that partnerships share with sole traders.

_____

_____

_____

5 Why is becoming a franchise now so popular as a way of starting, or expanding, a business?

_____

_____

_____

6   There are two kinds of limited liability company. What are they known as and what is the main difference between them, so far as raising money is concerned?

_____

_____

_____

7   Complete the following sentence.

Neither limited companies, nor registered charities, can do anything legally other than _____

_____

8   Complete the following sentence.

One of the principal differences between a public sector and a private sector organization is that the former is a _____ whereas the latter is a

_____

9   Fill in the blanks in the following sentence.

When considering a major _____ of their _____, senior managers should bear in mind the maxim that 'no _____ is generated inside a _____, only _____'.

Answers to these questions can be found on page 198.

7 Summary

- It is easier to see the signs of **poor** organization than of good organization – but the latter takes great effort behind the scenes to achieve.

- All organizations which succeed in the longer term must have:

  - a clear **purpose**;
  - a **structure** designed to suit that purpose;
  - excellent and continuing **management communications** at all levels to retain the commitment of all employees to the organization's purpose.

- The main types of organization are:

  - sole traders;
  - partnerships;
  - franchise organizations;
  - limited companies;
  - public sector, voluntary sector and 'self help' organizations.

- More than 80% of United Kingdom businesses employ ten people or less, and many of the new jobs and new ideas in the economy are generated by small businesses.

- Most large private sector businesses are limited companies that, legally speaking, have personalities distinct from that of their directors and members. They can, for example, make contracts, or be sued and prosecuted in their own name.

- It is as inexcusable for public and voluntary sector organizations to be inefficient as for a 'profit making' concern. Inefficiency reduces the amounts they can spend on public services and charitable purposes.

- There is no single organizational structure which is suitable for use in every circumstance. The main structures are:

  - hierarchical;
  - the wheel;
  - flat;
  - functional.

- As organizations grow, it becomes impossible for one person to carry out all the functions required and it is necessary to employ specialists in areas such as engineering, marketing, personnel and finance. Managing the specialists effectively then becomes a major part of senior management's role.

- The task of managers at every level, whatever their job title, is to provide support to the people who report to them and not to impose unnecessary administrative burdens on them.

Session B
The need for accounts

 1 Introduction

Money (or cash, or finance, or funds) is very important to all of us, both as private individuals and as members of organizations. It isn't that it is valuable in itself; its importance is in what it can buy and what it can do for us.

Trading organizations must keep detailed and accurate accounts if they are to stay in business at all, and if they hope to plan for the future in any meaningful way. For example, if manufacturers were approached to make a new product but did not have the right equipment to put the product together, they would have to buy new plant and machinery. If they did not know how much cash they had available, what was owing to them and how much they had to pay out in the next few weeks, how could they possibly agree to take on the contract?

Let's begin by looking at what money does for us.

2 How money is used

We are so familiar with money that it is easy to take it for granted and not analyse the ways in which we use it. But if you think about it, you will see the following issues.

- **Money acts as a medium of exchange.** Money enables people who make goods to obtain food, clothing and other wares. They sell their goods for money and then use the money to buy the things they need. Money enables them to exchange one thing for another.

- **Money acts as a store of wealth.** Money enables people to save or store money for 'rainy days', holidays, retirement and so on. Money is used to invest for the future.

- **Money acts as a means of deferred payment.** Money allows people to borrow and repay fixed amounts over a certain period. In other words, it allows them to buy something now, and put off or defer paying for it. They buy, say, a television now and pay for it over one or two years.

- **Money acts as a measure of values.** Money allows people to compare totally different things, such as a kilogram of apples and a pair of shoes. It is possible to do this by deciding what each is worth in money terms.

This last use of money, that enables one to apply a common measure of value to widely differing objects, is particularly useful. It means that the things you use at your workplace can be given a value in money terms, or 'costed'.

Try the following questions, before you move on.

Activity 17

10 mins

You have seen that money is used in at least four ways:

a as a medium of **exchange**;
b as a **store** of wealth;
c as a means of **deferred** payment;
d as a **measure** of values.

Decide how each of the following people are using money, by circling the appropriate letter (a), (b), (c) or (d), in each situation described below. Briefly describe the reasons for your selection.

1   John has a car and a house. He decides that together they are worth £175,000. Is he thinking of money in terms of (a), (b), (c) or (d) above?

2   Jack has won £2,000 on the lottery, and decides to put the money into a building society until he needs it. Is he thinking of money in terms of (a), (b), (c) or (d) above?

3   Janet borrows £1,000 from her father to buy a car. She agrees to pay the money back at £100 a month over 10 months. Is she thinking of money in terms of (a), (b), (c) or (d) above?

4   Diana sells her house for £150,000 and buys a smaller house for £130,000 and a car for £20,000. Is she thinking of money in terms of (a), (b), (c) or (d) above?

1   A car and a house are so different from each other that John can only group them together if he gives them a money value. So in this case he is using money as (d) a **measure** of values. If John's car was vintage or veteran he might combine the car and house as (b) a **store** of wealth.

You can see that the categories are not always clear cut. Different interpretations are possible.

2   Jack is saving money to use it later, so in this case he is using money as (b) a **store** of wealth. He is also using it as an investment for the future.

3   Janet's borrowing enables her to have the car now and pay for it over a period, so she is using money as a means of (c) **deferred** payment. She will also be exchanging the cash for the car.

4   Finally, Diana is able to exchange one item, her house, for a car and a smaller house. In this case she is using money as (a) a medium of **exchange.**

Whatever the way in which an organization uses money, it will need to record the transactions as proof of how it has used the money for all those interested in its operations.

3 The use of accounting records

Accounting records are kept by individuals, businesses, clubs, charities and non-profit organizations in order to monitor their financial positions. Accounting is the common language of business because it is used to describe the financial dealings of every kind of organization. Accounts are prepared from accounting records using the principles of accounting. We've just examined the way in which money serves a variety of purposes. We can look at accounting records, accounting and accounts in the same way.

There are a number of reasons why businesses keep accounting records and prepare accounts. An organization must:

- know what it owes;
- know what it is owed;
- know what it owns;
- be able to examine its activities to ensure that it makes a profit or works within a budget;
- be able to plan for the future.

In addition, certain organizations such as companies, charities and building societies are required by law to keep accounting records and prepare accounts. We will not look at legal requirements in this workbook.

The first three reasons for keeping accounting records are easily achieved by keeping a note of, or monitoring, transactions. The last two reasons are fulfilled by preparing accounts (or financial statements which we will look at later in this workbook).

3.1 Monitoring transactions

Activity 18

5 mins

Suppose you earn £300 per week and are paid at the end of the week. In reality you are owed £60 by the organization for which you work at the end of Monday, another £60 at the end of Tuesday and so on until Friday.

It's the same with the money you owe to others, such as the milkman and the newsagent. You may have milk and newspapers delivered, and pay what you owe at the end of the week, although bills aren't all as simple as this. Let's say that you owed the following amounts:

- Monday £30;
- Tuesday £35;
- Wednesday £45;
- Thursday £40;
- Friday £10;
- Saturday £20;
- Sunday £10.

Draw up your weekly account in the following table; the first entry is shown as an example.

	What you are owed	What you owe
Monday	£60	£30
Tuesday		
Wednesday		
Thursday		
Friday		
Saturday		
Sunday		
Totals		

You will know when you have to pay for say, your rent, as your landlord calls round at the same time each month and you make sure you have the cash available. Businesses do the same, and we will look at the timing of payments later.

The answer to this activity is on page 207.

Activity 19

5 mins

Haugh Limited owes £3,000 to Punton plc. Haugh Limited does not have enough cash to pay this debt at the moment. However, it is owed £3,000 by people who have bought goods from it on credit.

How can the directors of Haugh Limited decide when they will be able to repay the debt to Punton plc?

_____

_____

_____

The directors of Haugh Limited would want to know when the £3,000 it is owed will be paid. Until the cash comes in from its customers, it will clearly not be available to pass it on to Punton plc. So the directors will need to know the various dates when the cash will be coming in, particularly when the full amount is to be received. The directors can then promise Punton plc that they will be paid after a particular date. Of course, Haugh Limited will then be relying on its customers paying up when they say they will.

Organizations could have a number of debts and be owed money for many sales. This makes it even more important for its accounting records to be accurate so that they can manage to pay debts on time whenever possible.

What else could Haugh Limited have done?

- The company could default by not paying what it owes. (Not recommended!)
- It could borrow the money – it would then still owe £3,000, but to the bank, not Punton plc.
- It could sell something it owns – it could sell £3,000 worth of goods, or sell off a piece of land or equipment, for immediate payment so that it can pay the money on to Punton plc.

This suggests that the following are closely connected in the accounting records of Haugh Limited in this case:

- how much is **owned** by the company;
- how much is **owed** by the company;
- how much is **owed** to the company.

This applies equally to all organizations. A care provider must pay employees, business rates and other expenses on time; a charity may need to finance a homeless shelter by a specific date. And you can imagine the effects of the cash not being available at the right time on the customers and clients of such organizations.

3.2 Working to a budget

Now let's look at our fourth reason why a company keeps accounting records: to be able to examine its activities to ensure that it makes a profit or works within a budget. Again we'll take an example.

Activity 20 · 3 mins

Suppose your take-home pay this month is £1,000 and you have to make the following payments:

- housekeeping £400;
- mortgage £300;
- insurance £100;
- car loan £250.

It's clear that you don't have enough money to meet all your monthly payments. You are going to be short by £50.

From our last activity we know you could try to borrow the £50, or you could default on one of your payments, but this would be foolish! Next month, you'd have a worse problem – you would be £50 short again and also owe £50.

Make a brief note of how you might deal with this problem.

_____

_____

_____

It seems apparent that your income must rise or your spending must be reduced. You could do this by, for example:

- selling your car – if it covers the outstanding loan;
- cancelling your insurance – or changing to cheaper cover;
- cutting down on housekeeping;
- remortgaging so as to get a better rate of interest.

In order to avoid long-term debt your income must exceed your expenditure, and the same applies to any organization. In the long term no organization can survive if the money it receives – whether this be from sales, grants or even a donation from those who distribute the funds of the National Lottery – is less than the money it spends.

3.3 Making a profit

We can see that an organization cannot survive unless it has enough income to pay its expenses. So the fourth reason why a business must keep accounting records is to enable it to examine its day-to-day activities to ensure that it makes an excess of income over expenditure – known as a profit – or at least works within its budget.

Profit = Total income − Total expenditure

Organizations that do not make a profit will need to ensure that at the worst:

Total income = Total expenditure

This ensures survival. Often non-profit organizations will want to make a surplus, which is their equivalent of a profit. The difference is they don't usually have shareholders to pay dividends to, so the surplus is money for a 'rainy day'.

Activity 21

Suggest a couple of additional reasons why an organization should wish to make a profit or surplus.

_____

_____

There are various possibilities you may have suggested, such as:

■ to provide money to pay out to the owners as a reward for financing a business;
■ to build up money to replace equipment and machinery as it wears out;
■ to help the organization expand.

3.4 Planning

Suppose your monthly take-home pay is £1,000 and your monthly expenses are £950. This enables you to save £50 per month. Next year, you may want to go abroad on holiday, which will cost you £850. However, in the next twelve months you can only save £600.

In the same way, an organization's plans have to be based upon realistic forecasts of the money it will have available. And you saw from the last activity how important generating profits is in helping to put plans into action.

This is the fifth reason for keeping accounting records: to make it possible to plan for the future in a practical way.

Activity 22

5 mins

Amos Phiri expects his business to generate a profit of £42,000 in the next year and there are several ways he could deal with the profit:

1 he could pay his employees a bonus of 10% of their annual wages, which will cost £36,000;

2 he could buy himself a BMW car for £38,000;

3 he could purchase new machinery for £40,000 which it is expected will generate a further £10,000 profit each year;

4 he could keep all the profit in the bank in a deposit account just in case the business is less successful in the future.

Write down one point for and one point against each of the above possible courses of action.

1 For _____

Against _____

2 For _____

Against _____

3 For _____

Against _____

4 For _____

Against _____

There are a number of points you may have suggested. For instance, a bonus to employees might well encourage loyalty and retain staff, and they might work harder for Amos. But they might expect to receive a bonus in future years, and even include an amount for a bonus in their annual household budget. Or, they may feel that it would be better to include the amount in wages in future. Much depends on the present relationship between Amos and his employees.

As the business belongs to Amos, he would be within his rights to take out the money and buy a BMW. Clearly this would benefit him. But this might well cause resentment among the workforce who helped to generate the profit.

In both of the first two examples, money is going out of the business for good, and if the next year is not as successful, this could mean it gets into financial difficulties without anything to 'fall back on'.

The idea of purchasing more machinery to generate additional profits is attractive for the business and, if employees see this as a signal of job security, it could be well received by them too. If the plans are successful, there will be more to share out in the future. But, it does mean deferring rewards for employees and the owner to some future time. And both Amos and his workers might like some money now.

Finally, keeping the profit in a bank deposit account would help in case of future financial difficulties. But a greater profit is likely to be made if Amos uses the money in the business than would be obtained from interest paid on a deposit account.

Whenever a business makes plans, there will be disadvantages as well as advantages in each plan. Accounting helps to show the financial effects of the various options. And there is more to think about than purely financial matters, as you can see.

4 Accounting records and accounts

Earlier on we distinguished between accounting records on the one hand, and accounts (or financial statements) on the other. You may be wondering about the importance of this distinction.

Activity 23

Suppose you help your sister with her market stall business on a Saturday. She keeps a little notebook in which she jots down each transaction as it takes place. She buys her stock from four different suppliers as follows, and pays in cash as noted below:

Supplier A   £100
Supplier B   £250
Supplier C   £50
Supplier D   £175

On Saturday she sells all her goods to ten different customers, noting down the following amounts received in cash: £10, £75, £80, £65, £90, £115, £20, £25, £70, £45, £100.

She also makes a note of paying the market operator £25 cash, and giving you £20 cash for helping her.

Your sister thinks she had a good day. Try to answer this question quickly without using a calculator: did she have a good day?

Unless you have a fantastic head for numbers, you probably couldn't answer this question immediately with any degree of certainty. While your sister's notebook is a form of accounting record for what happened, the numbers don't mean very much listed out separately. What we need is a summary of the different transactions that took place, and this is why we record individual transactions in **accounting records** to produce summary **accounts.**

Using the information from the accounting records that we have been given, we can prepare the following accounts for your sister (for income, stock purchases, stall rent and wages):

Account	Transactions in accounting records £	Total £
Income	10 + 75 + 80 + 65 + 90 + 115 + 20 + 25 + 70 + 45 + 100	695
Expenditure:		
Stock purchases	100 + 250 + 50 + 175	(575)
Stall rent	25	(25)
Wages	20	(20)
Profit for the day		75

(It is an accounting convention to put amounts that are paid out, or owed, in brackets to show that they are to be deducted from the amounts received.)

So she did have a good day!

4.1 Source documents for accounting records

A business of any size can't hope to jot down its transactions in the way that your sister could for one quiet day's trading on her market stall. Also, notice that all your sister's transactions were settled immediately in cash. What if she hadn't paid immediately for her stock, or if she had agreed to wait for payment by one of her customers? How would these transactions be recorded?

Activity 24 · 5 mins

Your sister's market stall has done well recently and she has now rented premises, acquired a till and opened a business bank account. Some customers come in and pay by cash, but most use cheques, or are themselves businesses and ask for credit (that is, a delay between taking the goods and paying for them). She also persuades a few of her suppliers to allow her credit, so she doesn't have to pay immediately in cash for the stock she buys.

What kinds of document would you expect your sister to be dealing with:

For cash sales? _____

For cash purchases? _____

For sales on credit? _____

For purchases on credit? _____

What documents will your sister be dealing with if customers pay not in cash but by:

Cheque? _____

What documents will she be dealing with if she doesn't pay cash immediately to her suppliers?

_____

What documents will she be dealing with when her credit customers settle their bills?

_____

You may have had to think quite hard about some of these queries, but you could have come up with the following suggestions:

- source documents for cash sales: till roll, receipts to the customers;
- source documents for cash purchases: receipts (again), but from the suppliers for cash received;
- source documents for sales on credit: bills, or sales invoices from your sister to the customers;
- source documents for purchases on credit: bills (again), or invoices from the suppliers to your sister;
- source documents for receipts by cheque: cheques from customers to your sister;
- source documents for payments to credit suppliers: cheques from your sister to her suppliers.

You'll have noticed that I have called these items 'source documents'. This is because they are the source of the information on each transaction that will be recorded in your sister's accounting records, and which will eventually end up summarized in her accounts.

In the case of receipts given to her customers for a cash sale, and sales invoices to her credit customers, the source documents that your sister will keep in her records are copies of what is given away. She will keep the original of the receipt from her supplier for cash received, and of the invoice received from her supplier (often called a purchase invoice, though for the supplier of course it is a sales invoice). For cheques received from her customers she will have to note the details on a paying-in slip before handing the cheques over to her bank. And for cheques to her suppliers she will have to note the details on her cheque stub or counterfoil in her chequebook.

Activity 25

Try to find a copy of an invoice from a business that charges Value Added Tax (VAT). You will know that it is an invoice because it must say so by law. What details does it contain?

_____

_____

_____

An invoice with VAT has to contain certain information by law, and contains certain other information by convention. You might have noted down:

- supplier name, address and contact details;
- invoice number;
- customer name and address;
- VAT registration number;
- purchase order number or reference;
- delivery note number or reference;
- **date/tax point**;
- details of the goods or services being invoiced;
- charge for each item;
- rate of VAT applied to each item;
- trade, volume or bulk discount applied;
- **net total of goods/services**;
- **VAT amount**;
- **invoice total (often called the gross total)**;
- credit terms, including the period of credit allowed and whether there are any discounts for early payment;
- remittance advice, for sending back with the payment (often this is a bank giro credit form).

As you can see, there's a lot of information, but I've highlighted the most important information from an invoice that has to be entered in the accounting records.

The other important source document for accounting records is the credit note. Your sister would send one of these to her customer if the customer had returned goods to your sister. Similarly, she would receive a credit note from a supplier to whom she had returned goods.

5 How a business works

5.1 Business capital

Any business needs money to begin. Someone who sets up a cleaning service will need to pay for cleaning materials and, perhaps, advertising. A self-employed editor will need to pay for a computer, modem and printer at the very least. The permanent money used in a business is referred to as **capital** or **capital employed**. In a company, which is a particular legal form for a business, capital is provided in the form of **share capital**; the shares that make up the total share capital are purchased for cash by **shareholders.**

127485

Activity 26

10 mins

George and Mary would like to open a seaside cafe and are wondering what they could use for the opening capital. Which of the following might provide capital? Tick the appropriate box(es).

- Their savings.   ☐

- A loan from a bank.   ☐

- A gift from an uncle (or other relation).   ☐

- Cash from selling a share in the business to someone else.   ☐

- George's redundancy money from his last job.   ☐

Briefly explain why you might prefer one choice rather than the others.

_____

_____

_____

_____

Any of these sources might be acceptable, although it might be difficult to sell a share in a business that does not yet exist. Setting up in business is risky so George and Mary are likely not to want to use money they might need in the future, or that would involve difficulties with others if the cafe is not successful. So the best choices are probably savings and George's redundancy money, so long as some money remains for them in the event of failure. Providing the gift has 'no strings attached', this may be an even better choice. There would be a legal or moral liability to repay any loan, so if the cafe is unsuccessful George and Mary might not only lose the business but also have to repay the bank or an outsider.

Funds from the owner's own savings and gifts they receive are known as **owner's capital**. Loans, such as from a bank, are called **loan capital**. Accountants might say that a loan is not capital because it needs to be paid back to some-one outside the business. They would call it a **creditor**. In practice you will hear both terms used for loans.

5.2 Using capital

If George and Mary use their savings as owner's capital, how would they use it?

Activity 27

Look at the following list of items. Tick those which you think George and Mary might need.

- A building to work from. ☐

- A car or van for distribution. ☐

- Cash till. ☐

- Some form of machinery. ☐

In the space below, write down any other items you think may be needed.

_____

_____

_____

They will need a building for the cafe, which they may buy or rent, cooking equipment, perhaps an ice cream machine, tables and chairs, a cash till and a serving area. A car or van are probably not needed in a business like this. You may have thought of other examples.

> Fixed assets usually stay in an organization for more than a year.

A building, a car or van, equipment and other purchases of this kind will be bought with the intention of keeping them. Under normal circumstances they will not be for re-sale. As such, they are known as **fixed assets.**

Activity 28

If you start a business and have a building, a car or van, equipment and so on, you can begin work. Or can you? What else does a business need in order to trade? Write down two other things you think you may need.

_____

_____

You may have thought of a number of ideas. Perhaps they included:

- raw materials to be used to make goods with (food, in the case of George and Mary);
- other people to help you in your business;
- fuel, such as electricity.

All these items would have to be paid for. They are the things, and people, that are needed by the business in order to be able to sell goods or services. They are needed day to day and involve the business:

> Current assets and current liabilities are used up in an organization within a year.

- owning things like raw materials, which are part of the **current assets**;
- owing money to people such as employees and the electricity company, called **current liabilities** in accounting (they are also known as creditors);
- being owed money by its customers, known as **debtors**, who are also part of the **current assets**.

Current assets and current liabilities are grouped together and are called **working capital.**

So the owner's capital is used to obtain both the **fixed assets** and to provide the **working capital** (see the diagram, 'How owner's capital is used', below).

Working capital is the money circulating around a company. It flows out when it is used to buy materials and to employ people. It flows back in when goods or services are sold and cash is received.

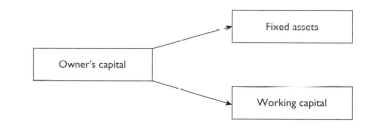

How owner's capital is used

Activity 29 · ⟨5 mins⟩

You identified various fixed assets that would be used in George and Mary's cafe. Would the following be current assets or current liabilities? Delete the one you think is incorrect.

- food;   Current asset/Current liability

- the amount owed to the supplier of
  the food;   Current asset/Current liability

- wages of a waitress;   Current asset/Current liability

- cash in the till.   Current asset/Current liability

All the items are used up within a year and so are current. George and Mary own the food and the cash in the till so these are current assets.

The amounts owed by the business to the supplier and the wages of a waitress are current liabilities.

Let's have a look at another couple of accounting terms you will meet regularly.

- People are often described as any organization's greatest asset. The accounting term for the cost of employing people is **labour**.
- When it is dark and cold you switch on lights and heating. In your business, you would also need to write letters to customers, send out invoices and so on. The costs of electricity, heating and items such as paper and stationery are called **overheads**. If you pay rent to a landlord then the rent is also an overhead.

So the picture of working capital can now be viewed as illustrated in 'Capital and working capital'. The large arrows indicate money flowing into and out of the business. The dotted lines indicate money flowing within the business.

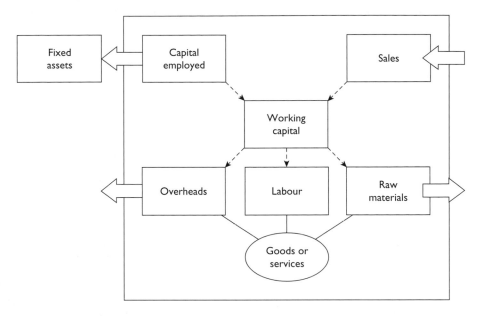

Capital and working capital

Activity 30

In George and Mary's cafe, they would expect to be paid in cash. But Saddiq sells electrical equipment, which is assembled in his factory, to a car manufacturer and sends out an invoice.

What problem might this cause for Saddiq's business?

_____

_____

_____

A delay between the delivery of goods and receipt of payment can cause businesses difficulties and make it difficult for them to pay their bills on time. Thi problem can put small, and even large, organizations out of business.

It is normal for there to be a delay – a period of credit – between receipt of goods and payment for them. At any one time Saddiq's business will usually be owed money. People who owe money to the business are called its **debtors**. (You may also see these called **accounts receivable**, particularly if you use computer software written outside the UK.)

In turn, the business will owe money to its **creditors**. (These are called **accounts payable** in many places outside the UK.)

Remember the difference between debtors and creditors. They are easy to confuse, but:

- debtors owe money to the business;
- the business owes money to creditors.

6 Cash flow

To stay in business and make a profit an organization must make sure that cash is available in the right quantity and at the right time to meet its commitments. To understand why this is so important you must get to grips with the fact that profit and cash are different.

When an item is sold for more than it cost to produce the seller makes a profit at the time of the sale. But if the sale is on credit then the profit is not really felt by the seller – or **realized** – until the cash is received from the debtor. During that period of credit the seller may simply run out of cash, so employees can't be paid, debts pile up and the whole thing ends in tears. This explains why so many companies that are 'profitable' fail – they are also, unfortunately, broke.

> A cash flow forecast is a statement which identifies expected cash receipts and payments in advance.

Without good control over cash there will be no future in which to try to make a profit. One technique that all businesses use to plan the money flowing in and out of the organization is a **cash flow forecast**. Once a forecast is made, it can then be compared with actual cash receipts and payments, week by week or month by month.

Let's look at an example. The Sharp Bakery has made a cash flow forecast of money coming in and going out of its business. Here is an extract:

Cash flow forecast – weeks 1 to 3

	Week 1 £'000	Week 2 £'000	Week 3 £'000	Week 4 £'000
Cash receipts (sales)				
Bread	150	150	150	
Cakes	250	250	250	
Total cash receipts	400	400	400	
Cash payment				
Ingredients	(106)	(106)	(106)	
Wages	(144)	(144)	(144)	
Overheads	(35)	(35)	(35)	
Van costs	(20)	(20)	(20)	
Total cash payment	(305)	(305)	(305)	
Net cash	95	95	95	
Cash balance B/F	Nil	95	190	
Cash balance C/F	95	190	285	

This statement is a forecast of the flows of cash in the first three weeks of trading of the bakery. Each expected item of cash receipts income is listed and, in this case, this is derived entirely from sales of bread and cakes. Then each expected item of cash payment expenditure is listed. In this case the costs are of making and delivering the bread and cakes.

The difference between receipts (cash in) and payments (cash out) is the forecast cash flow or **balance** or net cash at the end of each week's business. So, to take the first week, £305,000 of cash payments are deducted from £400,000 of cash receipts to give a cash balance of £95,000.

'Balance B/F' means the cash balance brought forward from the previous week and 'Balance C/F' means the cash balance carried forward to the next week. As Week 1 was the first week of business, no cash was brought forward.

Check your understanding of this cash flow statement by completing the next activity.

Activity 31

10 mins

a   Looking at the cash flow forecast above, what is the value of the forecast weekly cash sales?

_____

b   What is the forecast weekly wage bill?

_____

c   What are forecast weekly total cash costs?

_____

d   Assuming the figures for cash receipts and payment don't change from week to week, what is the net cash receipt for Week 4?

_____

e   Calculate the balance to be carried forward from Week 4 to Week 5.

_____

The correct figures are:

a   £400,000

b   £144,000

c   £305,000

d   £95,000

e   £380,000

We can see the business is forecasting a regular pattern of cash receipts and payments. In a more complicated situation, a business will have to plan for fluctuating receipts and payments.

This forecast can now be used to compare with actual receipts and payments. After the first week's trading, the actual receipts and payments are entered:

	Week 1		Week 2		Week 3		Week 4	
	Forecast £'000	Actual £'000	Forecast £'000	Actual £'000	Forecast £'000	Actual £'000	Forecast £'000	Actual £'000
Receipts								
Bread	150	140	150		150		150	
Cakes	250	220	250		250		250	
Total receipts	400	360	400		400		400	
Payments								
Ingredients	(106)	(112)	(106)		(106)		(106)	
Wages	(144)	(144)	(144)		(144)		(144)	
Overheads	(35)	(35)	(35)		(35)		(35)	
Van costs	(20)	(22)	(20)		(20)		(20)	
Total payments	(305)	(313)	(305)		(305)		(305)	
Net cash	95		95		95		95	
Cash balance B/F	Nil		95		190		285	
Cash balance C/F	95		190		285		380	

Activity 32 · 5 mins

In the table above, what is the actual cash balance at the end of Week 1?

_____

Write this figure into the cash flow forecast. The actual balance brought forward is nil, so what is the actual balance carried forward to Week 2?

_____

The correct figures are £47,000 at the end of Week 1 and, of course, this is the actual balance carried forward to Week 2. The closing balance of one period is the opening balance of the next.

The amount is calculated by deducting £313,000 from £360,000.

Activity 33 · 5 mins

The second week's actual trading figures for the Sharp Bakery are as follows:

		£'000
Receipts	Bread	150
	Cakes	200
Payments	Ingredients	105
	Wages	144
	Overheads	38
	Van	20

Add these figures to the table opposite and complete the calculation to find out the cash position at the end of week 2, writing it down below.

The cash balance at the end of Week 2 and carried forward for Week 3 is £90,000.

The comparison of actual figures with forecast ones gives management useful information on which to make decisions.

You can check the cash balance at the end of Week 2 in the table below.

At that stage you can see that the forecast cash balance was £190,000 and the actual position is £100,000 worse than that. You can see that sales have not been as high as expected although the expenditure is not vastly different.

	Week 1		Week 2		Week 3		Week 4	
	Forecast £'000	Actual £'000	Forecast £'000	Actual £'000	Forecast £'000	Actual £'000	Forecast £'000	Actual £'000
Receipts								
Bread	150	140	150	150	150		150	
Cakes	250	220	250	200	250		250	
Total receipts	400	360	400	350	400		400	
Payments								
Ingredients	(106)	(112)	(106)	(105)	(106)		(106)	
Wages	(144)	(144)	(144)	(144)	(144)		(144)	
Overheads	(35)	(35)	(35)	(38)	(35)		(35)	
Van costs	(20)	(22)	(20)	(20)	(20)		(20)	
Total payments	(305)	(313)	(305)	(307)	(305)		(305)	
Net cash	95	47	95	43	95		95	
Cash balance B/F	Nil	Nil	95	47	190		285	
Cash balance C/F	95	47	190	90	285		380	

Now let us take this one step further into weeks 3 and 4.

In Week 3, there is a Bank Holiday. Unfortunately, the bakery had not forecast any change in receipts because of this. During the same week a van crashed and had to be replaced, and an oven also developed a fault. The actual figures for Week 3 were therefore:

Receipts (sales)	Bread	£130,000	
	Cakes	£90,000	
Payments	Ingredients	£106,000	(normal orders for ingredients)
	Wages	£144,000	(Bank Holiday is paid for)
	Overheads	£44,000	(including oven repair)
	Van	£35,000	(including van purchase)

Activity 34

10 mins

Enter the figures for Week 3 into the cash flow forecast on page 61.

What is the actual cash balance carried forward at the end of Week 3? What does this tell you?

_____

_____

_____

You should have found that the actual cash balance at the end of Week 3 is negative. Receipt of £220,000 less payment of £329,000 gives an outflow of £109,000 cash for the week. And deducting the £109,000 outflow from the opening balance of £90,000 results in a negative balance of £19,000. Therefore, you can see that the amount recorded as the actual balance carried forward for Week 3 in the cash flow forecast below is (£19,000).

This means that the bakery would need to borrow money to cover the excess of payments over receipts or, perhaps, defer payment of some expenditure.

We have also entered figures for Week 4 below. This was a good week:

	Week 1		Week 2		Week 3		Week 4	
	Forecast £'000	Actual £'000	Forecast £'000	Actual £'000	Forecast £'000	Actual £'000	Forecast £'000	Actual £'000
Receipts (sales)								
Bread	150	140	150	150	150	130	150	150
Cakes	250	220	250	200	250	90	250	250
Total receipts	400	360	400	350	400	220	400	400
Payments								
Ingredients	(106)	(112)	(106)	(105)	(106)	(106)	(106)	(100)
Wages	(144)	(144)	(144)	(144)	(144)	(144)	(144)	(144)
Overheads	(35)	(35)	(35)	(38)	(35)	(44)	(35)	(35)
Van costs	(20)	(22)	(20)	(20)	(20)	(35)	(20)	(22)
Total payments	(305)	(313)	(305)	(307)	(305)	(329)	(305)	(301)
Net cash	95	47	95	43	95	(109)	95	99
Cash balance B/F	Nil	Nil	95	47	190	(90)	285	(19)
Cash balance C/F	95	47	190	90	285	(19)	380	80

Activity 35

5 mins

Now that you have been able to compare actual figures against the forecast ones for the first few weeks, what action, if any, might you consider taking if you were the owner of the bakery?

_____

_____

_____

_____

The bakery has seen that the actual cash flow does not always coincide with its forecasts. As you may agree, the bakery should take note of this, learn to plan a little better, and be careful to keep costs down, especially as they appear to be producing a lot of waste product by producing the same amount of bread and cakes whatever the sales receipts.

In particular, the bakery should remember that sales will be limited in short weeks and should aim not to be over-ambitious in its forecasts.

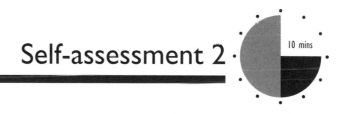

Self-assessment 2

10 mins

1   Complete the following statements by writing a suitable word or words in the space provided.

A company keeps accounting records because it needs to:

a know how much it _____ to other people;

b know how much it is _____ by other people;

c know the value of what it _____ ;

d know what changes need to be made if the money coming into the business is less than the amount _____ to other people;

e be able to _____ for the future.

2   Match each of the following four ways of using money with the **most** appropriate example.

a Medium of exchange.   (i)   Buying a bus ticket.
b Store of wealth.   (ii) An antique clock is valued at £750.
c Means of deferred payment.   (iii) Contributing to a pension plan.
d Measure of value.   (iv) Buying a coat using a credit card.

3   a State how the surplus or profit of an organization is calculated.

_____

_____

b Give **two** reasons why a business needs to make a profit.

_____

_____

4   a Why are source documents important for accounting?

_____

_____

_____

b What is the key information contained in:

1 a sales invoice? _____

2 a purchase invoice? _____

3 a cheque?_____

5   Match the terms on the left with the descriptions on the right.

a Owner's capital   (i)   Assets used within the business, and not
                             intended for resale.
b Fixed assets   (ii)   Capital provided by the business owner.
c Working capital   (iii) People the business owes money to.
d Labour   (iv)   People who owe the business money.
e Overheads   (v)   Current assets less current liabilities.
f Debtors   (vi)   The cost to the business of its employees.
g Creditors   (vii) The incidental expenses incurred in running
                             a business, including fuel and rent.

6   In the first two months of operation, Julia Ferguson had the following transactions:

May
  ■ Opening capital £450
  ■ Receipts from sales £1,040
  ■ Materials paid for £500
  ■ Overheads £200

June
  ■ Receipt from sales £990
  ■ Materials paid for £560
  ■ Overheads £210

When she started her business, Julia hoped to be able to purchase a second-hand delivery van for £1,000 at the start of July.

Identify and explain whether or not this is possible.

7   Briefly explain the problems that are likely to arise when a business decides to offer customers a six month interest free credit period after previously allowing customers only one month credit.
What are the benefits of making an offer like this?

Answers to these questions can be found on pages 199–201.

7 Summary

- The uses of money are as:

  - a medium of exchange;
  - a store of wealth and investment for the future;
  - a means of deferred payment (delayed payment over a period);
  - a common measure of value.

- Organizations keep accounting records to show:

  - how much they owe;
  - how much they are owed;
  - the value of what they own.

- Accounting records enable an organization to monitor day-to-day activities, in order to ensure that expenditure is kept below income. Without this monitoring and control, it would not be possible for the organization to make plans or, in the long term, to survive.

- Accounting principles are used to prepare accounts (or financial statements) from accounting records.

- Source documents, such as receipts for cash paid and received, invoices and cheques, provide key information on the amounts to be recorded for each transaction entered into by an enterprise. Accounting records allow us to record these individual transactions. Accounts are prepared from accounting records and summarize all the individual transactions.

- Capital comes from:

  - the owners, when it is known as owners' capital;
  - issuing shares to other people, when it is known as share capital;
  - loans, when it is known as loan capital. Loans have to be paid back and are also known as creditors.

- Capital is:

  - invested in fixed assets, such as buildings, which are not normally for resale;
  - used as working capital which circulates in the business and is used to produce eventual sales of goods or services. Working capital comprises raw materials and other current assets as well as current liabilities.

- Debtors owe money to the business, while creditors are owed money by the business.

- Overheads are the general expenses of running a business, for example heat, light, rent and telephone.

- A cash flow forecast is a way of planning, monitoring and controlling what is likely to happen in the coming period so far as receipts and payments are concerned. Even a forecast that proves to be somewhat inaccurate can be used to anticipate problems and plan for expected shortages.

Session C
Financial information

1 Introduction

In this session we will look at the way accounting procedures are used in organizations to prepare the year-end financial statements, such as the published annual reports and accounts of companies.

These annual reports represent an organization's effort to the outside world and provide useful information for shareholders, potential investors, lenders, employees and others.

How much of your pension fund is invested in companies quoted on the London Stock Exchange? How much do you know about them? Do you want to know more?

2 Cash accounting versus profit accounting

We saw in Session B that the cash flow forecast looks at transactions in terms of cash flow. In each month, a business assesses how much it will pay out as cash and how much it will receive in. This means that it can plan to have enough of its lifeblood, cash, to survive and grow.

Activity 36

Johnson Ltd makes sales of £10,000 in its first month of trading, November, and incurs expenses of £6,500. Only 50% of its customers settle their bills in November, and Johnson Ltd pays only 10% of its expenses in the month.

By how much do Johnson Ltd's cash receipts exceed its cash payments for November?

_____

_____

By how much does Johnson Ltd's income (sales) exceed its expenses in November? What is this figure usually called?

_____

_____

Explain why the two figures you have calculated are different.

_____

_____

You should have calculated that Johnson Ltd received cash of £5,000 (£10,000 × 50%) in November, and paid out only £650 (£6,500 × 10%). In cash terms, therefore, its receipts exceeded its payments by £4,350. But Johnson Ltd sold only £3,500 more than it incurred as expenses in November (£10,000–£6,500). The figure of £3,500 is its profit for November.

Don't worry if you struggled a little to explain the difference. It comes from the fact that the figure of £3,500 is calculated by taking into account _both_ sales and purchases that have been settled in cash _and_ those that have not. If Johnson Ltd made no transactions in December, but simply waited for the cash to roll in while paying its bills, by the end of December it would have received only £3,500 more than it paid out, as all the November transactions would have been realized in cash. The fact that its receipts and payments situation looks better than its income and expenses position at the end of November is purely down to the fact that Johnson Ltd is better at getting money in from its debtors than it is at paying its creditors.

Looking at income and expenses, whether realized or unrealized in the form of cash, is called **profit (or accruals) accounting**, and is the principle that underlies the financial information that we will examine in the rest of this session.

3 The profit and loss account

You have seen that by making up a cash flow forecast for the *future* on the basis of likely receipts and payments, and monitoring it weekly or monthly, a business has a way of planning and controlling its lifeblood, which is the availability of cash.

An organization measures its *past* operations through a **profit and loss account**. This is a summary of a company's financial performance over the last year, rather than how it is likely to operate in the future.

A profit and loss account shows what a business has earned in total, known as **income** or **revenue**, against what it has spent, known as **expenses**. Where revenue exceeds expenses, the business has made a **profit**. Where expenses exceed income, the business has made a **loss.**

A simplified profit and loss account might look like this:

	£	£
Hillside Company Limited		
Profit and loss account for the year ended 31 March		
Sales		100,000
Less cost of goods sold		(40,000)
Gross profit		60,000
Labour	20,000	
Overheads	20,000	(40,000)
Net profit for the year		£20,000

The right-hand column shows how expenses (in brackets) are deducted from income, and the resulting profit figures. The centre, numerical, column shows how sub-totals are made up.

Two important features in the account are as follows:

- **Gross profit**: this measures the company's success at buying and selling goods or services. The part of the financial statement in which gross profit is calculated is often called the **trading account**.

- **Net profit**: this measures the success of the company's operations for the year. The costs of wages and salaries and other overheads are deducted from the gross profit to arrive at the net profit.

There are several important differences between the two types of accounting we have looked at so far (profit accounting and cash accounts), and they affect the profit and loss account. The main ones are listed in the table below:

	Profit accounting	**Cash accounting**
Sales	As long as invoices have been sent out, a profit and loss account recognizes them as money coming in even before the cash has been received.	Cash is only recognized when it has been received.
Fixed assets	When a fixed asset is sold, it is the profit or loss on the sale which is accounted for – that is, the cash received from the cost of the fixed asset.	When a fixed asset is sold, the total cash value of the sale is accounted for – the cash available.
Expenses	Invoices that have been received, and even goods or services that have been received but without an invoice, are recognized as money going out even before the cash has been paid.	What is recognized is what is actually paid.

3.1 Cost of goods sold

Trading businesses buy goods at one price, put them in stock and later hope to sell them at a higher price. To find out how much stock they have at the end of one financial year, they carry out stocktaking. Stocktaking is done to arrive at the true stock position at the end of a trading year, known as the **closing stock**. This will also be the value of stock for the beginning of the next year, and therefore is referred to as the **opening stock** for that year.

Some organizations have end-of-year stocktaking where all the stock is counted. Others use perpetual stocktaking where continual records, on computer, are kept and checks on stock are made throughout the year.

In the case of the Hillside Company, the end of the financial year is March. The figure for the cost of goods sold was found by taking the opening stock figure, adding materials purchased during the year (whether paid for or not), and taking away the closing stock figure:

	£
Opening stock	10,000
Add purchases	50,000
Less closing stock	(20,000)
Cost of goods sold	40,000

Activity 37

10 mins

Here are the figures for a year's trading to 31 March for Straton Limited, calculated on a profit accounting basis (that is, ignoring whether or not sales or expenses have been settled in cash).

	£
Sales	60,000
Opening stock	10,000
Purchases	20,000
Closing stock	5,000
Overheads	10,000
Wages	15,000

Produce a profit and loss account for Straton Limited. What are the gross and net profits?

_____

_____

_____

_____

_____

_____

_____

_____

_____

_____

_____

_____

_____

_____

_____

_____

_____

The answer to this activity can be found on page 207.

3.2 Deductions from profit

The profit and loss accounts we have looked at so far have been simplified ones. There are other expenses in a business which must be taken into account.

Activity 38 · 5 mins

Think about other expenses that your organization has in relation to its fixed assets, and write down **two** below:

_____

_____

You may have mentioned such expenses as insurance, repairs and running costs. An important item you may not have included in your list is **depreciation.**

Depreciation is a feature of profit accounting that does not appear as such in cash accounts. This is because it is a way of charging the cost of a fixed asset to the profit and loss account, reducing profit over a period of some years.

Say Barnard Ltd bought a large mechanical digger for £50,000 and paid for it in cash. It planned to use the digger in its business for twenty years.

In cash accounting, this fixed asset purchase would appear as an increase in payments of £50,000 in the year it was paid for. In profit accounting, however, the digger would be depreciated, so that each year of its useful life receives some charge for the fixed asset. Depreciation might be in equal instalments over the twenty years of its useful life, so each year – even the year it was bought – receives the same charge of £50,000/20 = £2,500. Or it might be by some other method, which makes a higher charge in earlier years when the digger is more effective.

You can see that charging depreciation over a period, rather than the full cost at one time will make a great deal of difference to a company's apparent profitability. Remember, though, that the cash is still gone. **Depreciation does not affect cash flow; fixed asset purchases do.**

Other 'deductions' you will see in a company profit and loss account include:

- tax against profits levied by government, such as corporation tax;
- dividends to be paid to shareholders.

Shareholders, who invest in a company by buying shares, are part owners of the company. If the business does badly, they may lose their money. They therefore expect a reward from the business when it does well, to compensate for the risk they are taking.

Dividends are seen as ways of sharing out the profit earned, known as **appropriations of profit.**

Let's continue the profit and loss account for Straton Limited using some slightly different terms.

	£	£
Straton Limited		
Profit and loss account for the year ended 31 March		
Turnover		60,000
Cost of sales		(25,000)
Gross profit		35,000
Operating expenses		
Wages	(15,000)	
Overheads	(10,000)	
Rates	(2,000)	
Interest on loan	(2,000)	
Depreciation	(3,000)	(32,000)
Profit on ordinary activities before taxation		3,000
Tax on profit on ordinary activities		(400)
Profit on ordinary activities after taxation		2,600
Dividends paid		(1,000)
Retained profit		1,600

This is the sort of structure or layout you will see in your own or another company's annual report and accounts, although you may notice some differences. For example, other items may be shown. Note that in the above **turnover** is another name for sales, and **profit on ordinary activities before taxation** is the same as net profit.

The profit figure before tax is usually called the **pre-tax profit**. The **retained profit** is the final surplus which a business can use to reinvest in itself for growth.

3.3 Income and expenditure accounts

So far the examples we've looked at have concentrated on businesses of various sizes, that are aiming to make a profit. What accounting principles hold true for non-profit organizations? They don't aim to make a profit, so is profit accounting appropriate?

In fact the same accounting principles hold true for non-profit organizations as for profit making ones, so profit accounting is appropriate. The reason is this: if accounts only showed cash transactions (actual receipts and payments) then an organization could easily manipulate its figures at a particular year end simply by not paying its bills until after the year end. Nobody reading the financial statements would know about the unpaid liabilities. This would not be a good way for any organization, a business or a non-profit one such as a club, a society, a charity or a public sector body, to present its affairs.

There are some differences of terminology, however. A non-profit organization presents an **income and expenditure account**, rather than a profit and loss account. Instead of a profit it might report a **surplus of income over expenditure**; instead of a loss there might be a **deficit**, or an **excess of expenditure over income.**

There are also considerable differences in operations.

Activity 39

15 mins

Take a look at the end-of-year financial statements of your own organization and two or three others, say, a bank or building society, a club or a charity.

Look at the profit and loss accounts or income and expenditure accounts. Note down, on a separate sheet of paper, the various names used for:

- sales or turnover;
- gross profit;
- net profit;
- retained profit.

You now have a greater understanding of the terminology used in different organizations and, in particular, your own. This will help you in understanding how resources have been used and the financial results of their use. You may have seen **fees**, donations, grants, subscriptions or **takings** for sales or turnover; **trading profit** for gross profit; **surplus of income over expenditure** for net profit; **undistributed profit** or **undistributed surplus** for retained profit, and so on.

Whilst looking for the specific features of profit and loss statements and income and expenditure accounts, you probably saw a number of different terms used for types of expenditure which represent the use of resources. If you have extra time to study these, this will improve your overall understanding of financial information.

4 The balance sheet

The **balance sheet** is a 'snapshot' of a company's assets and liabilities at a specific moment in time, say 31 May, which tells us where the money is used and where it came from.

One difference between a balance sheet and a profit and loss account (or income and expenditure account) is that the latter is a statement of what has happened over a period of time – usually a year.

Before moving on let's remind ourselves about some terms we have already met.

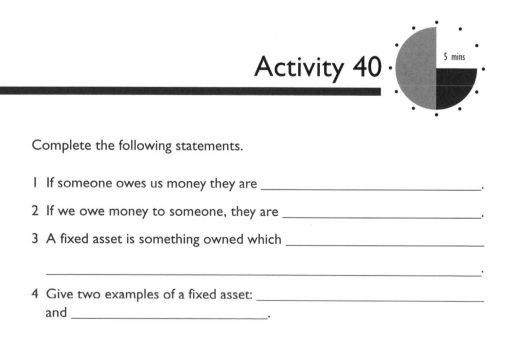

Activity 40 · 5 mins

Complete the following statements.

1 If someone owes us money they are _____.

2 If we owe money to someone, they are _____.

3 A fixed asset is something owned which _____

_____.

4 Give two examples of a fixed asset: _____
   and _____.

This is a revision of your earlier work; if you had any difficulties, you should refer back and check your previous studies.

1 If someone owes us money they are DEBTORS.

2 If we owe money to someone, they are CREDITORS.

3 A fixed asset is something owned which is normally not for sale.

4 Examples of fixed assets are: a car; a computer bought for use in the business; machinery; a building; … anything purchased for use in an enterprise over a period longer than a year.

4.1 Assets and liabilities

To know how you stand financially you need to list what you **owe**, what is **owed to you** and what you **own**. In businesses the same applies and we use terms such as **assets** and **liabilities** in our lists.

A personal computer, an article produced in the factory for sale, cash in the bank, or money owed by a customer are all of value to a business, because they can be used by the business or will bring money into the business.

Assets are things that are of value to a business.

Other things dealt with in financial accounts, such as money owed to a supplier, or business rates owed to the council, represent claims against the business.

Claims against a business are called liabilities.

Activity 41   5 mins

Look at each of these items and decide whether it is an ASSET or a LIABILITY. Delete the one you think is incorrect.

a Debtors.   ASSET/LIABILITY
b Creditors.   ASSET/LIABILITY
c Cash in the bank.   ASSET/LIABILITY
d Buildings.   ASSET/LIABILITY
e Machinery.   ASSET/LIABILITY
f Vehicles.   ASSET/LIABILITY

g   Goods for sale.   ASSET/LIABILITY
h   Corporation tax.   ASSET/LIABILITY
i   Overdraft.   ASSET/LIABILITY

The ASSETS in the list are:

a   Debtors (people who owe us money).
c   Cash in the bank.
d   Buildings.
e   Machinery.
f   Vehicles.
g   Goods for sale.

There are three LIABILITIES:

b   Creditors (people we owe money to).
h   Corporation tax.
i   Overdraft.

Earlier in this workbook we talked briefly about current and fixed assets. You will remember that fixed assets are worth money and will not normally be sold or converted into cash. The assets that are already cash, such as cash in the bank, or that are going to be turned into cash very quickly, like debtors, are current assets.

Activity 42 · 5 mins

Tick which of the following assets are fixed assets.

a   Debtors.   ❑
b   Cash in the bank.   ❑
c   Buildings.   ❑
d   Machinery.   ❑
e   Vehicles.   ❑
f   Goods for sale.   ❑

Fixed assets are held for the longer term and include:

c   Buildings.
d   Machinery.
e   Vehicles.

The other assets – debtors, cash in the bank and goods for sale – are all **current assets.**

You will also see **current liabilities** in the accounts of organizations. Typical examples are trade creditors (suppliers), a bank overdraft and, in a company, the tax and dividends owing. Tax is a private matter for a sole trader or partners.

There are also **long-term liabilities**. These are claims against the business such as:

■ loans from a bank or elsewhere that are repayable in more than a year;

■ amounts owed under leases.

We saw earlier that **owner's capital** is a kind of long-term liability. This is because these funds will eventually, in theory, have to be repaid to the owners, just like a bank loan will have to be repaid. And just as the bank accepts interest as the 'price' of the loan over time, owners seek some sort of return on the capital they have provided.

For sole traders and partners, the return they receive is called **drawings** (literally, they draw money out of the business). Shareholders in a company receive **dividends** as their return on capital. (The fact that shareholders in companies that are listed on a stock exchange can make a profit individually, by selling their shares at a higher price than they bought them for, is basically a bonus that has little or nothing to do with the company.)

Sometimes you will hear the term '**equity**' used in the context of company shareholders. All this means is that each shareholder of, say, a £1 share has an equal right to receive a return on that £1 share as any other shareholder of a £1 share.

4.2 Preparing a balance sheet

At least once a year, and often more frequently, the assets and liabilities of a business are listed in a statement called a **balance sheet.**

A simple, but incomplete, balance sheet may look like this (eventually the totals on the left and the right sides will be the same, or 'balance'):

Jute Jewels Limited

Balance sheet as at 31 March

	£	£		£
Fixed assets				
Buildings	4,000			
Machinery	800			
Vehicles	1,000			
		5,800	(we will put an entry in this section shortly)	
Current assets			*Current liabilities*	
Stock	1,000		Creditors	500
Debtors	1,000			
Cash at bank	500	2,500		
		£8,300		£500

This balance sheet is incomplete. It is easy to tell this fact, because it doesn't yet balance – the two sides are not equal. Every balance sheet must show that the total assets equal the total liabilities plus capital.

If we deduct the immediate claims against the business (the current liabilities) from the things that are of value to the business (the assets) in this balance sheet, we are left with £7,800, which is called the **capital employed** in the business.

Capital employed is total assets less current liabilities.

Depending on the type of business, capital employed can comprise:

■ long-term liabilities – bank loans, leases, debentures (long-term loans to bodies other than banks);
■ owner's capital.

We can now complete the balance sheet:

Jute Jewels Limited

Balance sheet as at 31 March

	£	£		£
Fixed assets			Capital	7,800
Buildings	4,000			
Machinery	800			
Vehicles	1,000			
		5,800		
Current assets			*Current liabilities*	
Stock	1,000		Creditors	500
Debtors	1,000			
Cash at bank	500	2,500		
		£8,300		£8,300

Now you can see why it is called a balance sheet: the **total assets balance the total liabilities.**

Activity 43

10 mins

Decide which of the following are assets and which are liabilities. Then enter them as appropriate in the balance sheet below. Calculate the capital employed (total assets minus current liabilities) and enter the figure in the right place on the balance sheet.

		Hint
Debtors	10,000	There are:
Creditors	12,000	
Cash at bank	800	three fixed assets
Factory	50,000	three current assets
Machinery	8,000	one current liability
Vehicles	1,000	
Goods for sale	3,000	

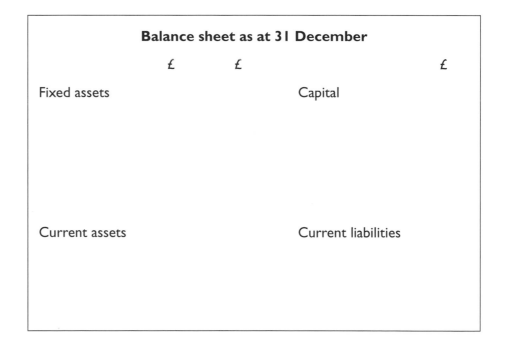

Balance sheet as at 31 December

	£	£		£
Fixed assets			Capital	
Current assets			Current liabilities	

Let's see how you did. You should have added up the total assets and subtracted the creditors to arrive at capital. Did you?

Balance sheet as at 31 December

	£	£		£
Fixed assets			Capital	60,800
Factory	50,000		(balancing figure)	
Vehicles	1,000			
Machinery	8,000	59,000		
Current assets			*Current liabilities*	
Goods for sale	3,000		Creditors	12,000
Debtors	10,000			
Cash at bank	800	13,800		
		£72,800		£72,800

You'll notice that the total of the assets side of the balance sheet is the same as the total of the liabilities side.

A balance sheet does not tell us what a business is worth. Instead, it tells us how the business is financed.

In the previous activity, for example, the business is made up of three different fixed assets and three different current assets. These assets are financed by £60,800 worth of capital and £12,000 worth of credit at the time the balance sheet is drawn up.

4.3 The balance sheet and the profit and loss account

You may be wondering why – if the balance sheet is a snapshot and the profit and loss account (or, indeed, the income and expenditure account) covers a period of a year or so – the two statements are always presented together.

The reason is that the two parts are very closely linked, namely by the capital section in the balance sheet, to the retained profit in the profit and loss account.

Basically the retained profit for the period (shown in the profit and loss account) is added to the owner's capital (shown in the previous balance sheet) to arrive at the new balance sheet. The fact that the enterprise has made money, be it a profit or a surplus, in the period causes the total assets less current liabilities – often called the net assets – to increase. In turn this means there is an increase in the capital section.

See for yourself, by completing the activity below. Note the slightly different layout of the balance sheet, which separates capital employed completely from total assets less current liabilities, or **net assets**. The vertical format is also a common presentation. Finally, the accumulated retained profit over years is usually referred to as the **profit and loss reserve.**

Activity 44 · 15 mins

At 1 January the balance sheet of Crombie Ltd was as follows:

Crombie Ltd	
Balance sheet as at 1 January	
	£
Total assets	100,000
Current liabilities	(30,000)
Net assets	70,000
Share capital	20,000
Total profit retained in previous years (profit and loss reserve)	50,000
Capital employed	70,000

By 31 December Crombie Ltd had generated a retained profit for the year, as shown in its profit and loss account, of £15,000. Total assets had increased by £35,000, and current liabilities by £20,000.

Fill in the spaces in the balance sheet below.

Crombie Ltd

Balance sheet as at 31 December

	£
Total assets	
Current liabilities	_____
Net assets	_____
Share capital	20,000
Profit and loss reserve	50,000
Retained profit for the year	_____
Capital employed	_____

Did your balance sheet balance? Simply by adding the figures given to those in the brought forward balance sheet, you should have come up with the following balance sheet.

Crombie Ltd

Balance sheet as at 31 December

	£
Total assets	135,000
Current liabilities	(50,000)
Net assets	85,000
Share capital	20,000
Profit and loss reserve	50,000
Retained profit for the year	15,000
Capital employed	85,000

Before we leave this topic, consider briefly how Crombie Ltd's balance sheet would be affected if its shareholders had introduced £5,000 cash into the business (in return for shares).

The effect of this would simply be to increase net assets by £5,000 and to increase share capital by £5,000. The balance sheet totals would be £90,000 instead of £85,000.

However complicated a set of financial statements may look on the surface – and they can look very complicated indeed – you have now covered the basic principles which underlie their purpose and their preparation.

4.4 The balance sheet and the income and expenditure account

We need one last word on non-profit organizations. You will remember that an income and expenditure account will show a surplus of income over expenditure, or a deficit. Where does this appear on the organization's balance sheet?

The capital section of a non-profit organization's balance sheet is where it differs from those for businesses. These organizations have assets and liabilities just like a business, but instead of share capital or owner's capital, they have **funds or reserves**. There is a lot of variety in the terminology used for these funds, depending on the type of organization and its history. Below are some examples:

- founder's fund;
- endowment fund;
- building fund;
- bursary reserve;
- life fund;
- accumulated fund or reserve.

You may have found others when you looked at examples in earlier activities.

Some of these funds might be of a fixed amount, say where the founders of a charity gave it a fixed amount as its *founder's fund*. Some may be permanent in nature but can increase when certain payments are received by the organization, such as an *endowment fund* or a *bursary reserve*. Some may be set up with a particular objective in mind and be increased with surpluses and reduced with deficits until the objective is fulfilled, such as a *building fund*. Some may be required by the organization's constitution or by law, as a way of showing the amount of specific inflows of cash to the organization over time, such as a *life fund* in a life insurer. And some may simply be the equivalent of the profit and loss reserve in a business – the accumulated reserve.

5 Financial indicators

You have seen that a great deal of information is available from financial statements. However, you may wonder how this information can be used.

One answer is that it can be used to analyse companies to discover how healthy they are. In this session, we will look at a few important ratios, that is, measures or indicators of the performance of a business.

Whenever a bank is approached for a loan, or a pension fund is considering investing in the Stock Exchange, they will calculate a number of ratios to give them an idea about the performance of the organizations which are potentially going to get their money. Analysis by ratios helps them estimate the risks they will be taking.

You and your work team, the human assets of a company, do not appear in a balance sheet, either as assets or liabilities! However, you bring your skills, knowledge and experience to work and are key to a company's performance. Almost every part of an organization contributes to the control of current assets and minimizing of current liabilities, whether you are in planning, production, marketing, stock control, credit control or whatever. So, financial indicators are a measure of you, your team, and your management's performance.

Financial indicators can be calculated for a business as a whole, using positioned financial statements, or for parts of it. The latter approach means that the performance of individual managers can be measured.

The most commonly used indicators involve ratios. A ratio is a relationship between one number and another. If one work team has twelve people and another has eight people, the ratio of their numbers could be expressed in any of the following ways:

as $12:8$ *   or as* $\dfrac{12}{8}$ *   or as* $3:2$ *   or as* $\dfrac{3}{2}$ *   or as* $1.5:1$ *   or as* 1.5 *to* 1

Financial indicators are usually presented in one of the last two forms in the list above.

We shall look at some key financial measures of business performance, discussing liquidity (the ability to pay debts) and profitability.

5.1 Current ratios (liquidity)

You will remember that current assets are cash or nearly cash. Current liabilities are debts which have to be paid soon. A wise business will have enough current assets to ensure that they can pay current liabilities.

This idea gives us an important ratio or test called the **current ratio:**

$$\text{Current ratio} = \frac{\text{Current assets}}{\text{Current liabilities}}$$

If we want to know if a business is **solvent**, that is whether it can cover its debts, we would calculate the current ratio.

The current ratio is also called the **working capital ratio** because it compares the different aspects of working capital: current assets and current liabilities.

> The main reason for business failure is the inability to pay debts when due, because of lack of liquid cash. Such a business is **insolvent**.

Activity 45

5 mins

In the balance sheet for Lee Lay Chin, the current assets are £13,800 and the current liabilities are £12,000.

■ What is her current ratio?

_____

_____

_____

■ Do you think her business is solvent?

_____

_____

_____

_____

The current ratio is $\dfrac{£13,800}{£12,000} = 1.15$ to 1, so the business is solvent. A ratio of 1:1 or higher would mean it had enough current assets to pay all its immediate liabilities.

What we cannot guarantee, of course, is that the current assets, such as stock and debtors, can be turned into cash quickly enough to pay off the current liabilities when they are due. Customers supplied with goods and services on credit tend to take a month to pay generally, and stocks are likely to take even longer to turn into cash. If a business generally sells goods on credit, it will first need to sell the goods and then collect from the debtors who buy the goods before seeing the cash.

Therefore, we have a sharper test of solvency called the **quick ratio** or **'acid test'**. We take away stock from current assets and that gives us the **quick assets**. These are the assets which can be turned into cash quickly or are cash already.

$$\text{Acid test} = \frac{\text{Current assets} - \text{Stock}}{\text{Current liabilities}}$$

Activity 46 · 5 mins

Assume that Lee Lay Chin has stock valued at £3,000 in her current assets. What is her quick ratio?

Here, the calculations are:

$$\text{Quick ratio} = \frac{£13,800 - £3,000}{£12,000} = 0.9:1$$

This would still be considered as a healthy position – but only just! If you read textbooks on this subject, you are likely to see that recommended levels for these ratios are:

■ current ratio 2 :1;
■ quick ratio 1:1.

But much depends on the type of business. A supermarket turns its stock into cash very quickly and will usually have money available to pay its debts. It can survive on much lower ratios than, say, a manufacturer of luxury yachts who would have plenty of cash each time a yacht was sold, but would be building up stock for most of the time as each yacht is put together. To be truly solvent a yacht manufacturer might need a current ratio of 4 :1, 5:1 or more.

The best way to check solvency is to use both these ratios and a cash flow forecast (which we looked at in Session B) so you would get a good view of how the cash is flowing through the organization to meet liabilities.

To use ratio analysis properly, an accountant would:

Various books are available listing ratios for different industries and sizes of business.

■ compare an organization's ratios with those of other organizations in the same line of business;
■ compare the ratios with a known standard for an industry, if there is one.

5.2 Profit margin (profitability)

You might want to look at the profitability of sales in your business. This is called the profit margin and indicates what return a business is making as a result of its efforts.

For this we go to the profit and loss account and look at profit in relation to sales (revenue or turnover).

This indicator or ratio is expressed as a percentage (%):

$$\text{Profit margin} = \frac{\text{Profit before tax}}{\text{Sales revenue}} \times 100$$

Profit margin is also known as the **net profit percentage**.

Activity 47

5 mins

In the profit and loss account of Straton Limited which you saw earlier, the pre-tax profit was £3,000 and sales revenue was £60,000. What is the profit margin?

_____

_____

_____

_____

_____

The profit margin of Straton Limited is:

$$\frac{£3,000}{£60,000} \times 100 = 5\%$$

So, for every £1 of sales, the company made 5p net profit.

Again, to make sense of this indicator you would need to compare this with earlier results of the company and with the typical results for the industry. It is this comparison with the past, with other organizations, and with industry standards, which makes ratio analysis useful.

Activity 48

5 mins

Here are two consecutive years' results for Network Ltd and Bryn Ltd.

In year 1, Network Ltd has
sales of	£100,000
pre-tax profits of	£7,000

In year 2, it has
sales of	£120,000
pre-tax profits of	£8,000

In year 1, Bryn Ltd has
sales of	£400,000
pre-tax profits of	£23,000

In year 2, it has
sales of	£380,000
pre-tax profits of	£22,000

1   What is the profit margin of Network Ltd for each year?

_____

_____

_____

2   What is the profit margin of Bryn Ltd for each year?

_____

_____

_____

3   Which of the companies has improved its profit margin?

_____

_____

1 Network Ltd's profit margin is:

$$\frac{\text{Profit before tax}}{\text{Sales revenue}} \times 100 = \frac{7}{100} \times 100 = 7\% \text{ in Year 1}$$

and

$$\frac{8}{120} \times 100 = 6.67\% \text{ in Year 2}$$

2 Using the same formula, Bryn Ltd's profit margin is 5.75% in Year 1, and 5.79% in Year 2.

3 Bryn Ltd has improved its profit margin while that of Network Ltd has fallen.

5.3 Return on capital (profitability)

If you were thinking about investing in another business you would be interested in the **return on capital employed (ROCE)**. This shows how well the business uses the money invested in it.

The ROCE ratio is expressed as a percentage (%):

$$\text{Return on capital employed} = \frac{\text{Profit before tax}}{\text{Capital employed}} \times 100$$

Pre-tax profit is the same as the profit figure you used for the profit margin and comes from the profit and loss account. Capital employed is obtained from the balance sheet. It is calculated as capital plus reserves, or you will get the same figure by taking away current and long-term liabilities from total assets.

Activity 49 ·

5 mins

The capital employed in The Orange Company Ltd is £860,000. Its pre-tax profit is £65,000. What is the return on capital employed for the company?

_____

_____

_____

EXTENSION 2
If you would like to look at financial indicators in greater depth, take a look at *Business Accounting* by Alan Sangster and Frank Wood.

The ROCE (figures in £'000) is:

$$\frac{£65}{£860} \times 100 = 7.56\%$$

As with other ratios, the typical return on capital employed for a particular industry may differ widely from the ROCE in another industry. Generally, ratios relating to profits and returns reflect the risks in different organizations. An investor would expect a higher profit margin and return to compensate for the risk of losing everything.

Self-assessment 3 ·

20 mins

1   Draw up a profit and loss account for Lester Limited using the following information. The company trading year ends on 31 December. Use the framework provided. (All figures are in £'000.)

a   Cash sales were £352.
b   Credit sales were £400.
c   Stock at the beginning of the year was valued at £20.
d   Stock at the end of the year was valued at £70.
e   Purchases during the year came to £520.
f   Operating expenses, apart from stock, came to £120.
g   The company paid interest of £12 on loans.
h   Depreciation was calculated at £40.
i   Taxation is at a rate of 20% on profit.
j   The dividend was £4.

```
                    Lester Limited

    Profit and Loss Account for the year ended 31st December

                              £'000              £'000
Sales
Cost of goods sold
Gross profit
Overhead expenses



Profit before tax
Tax
Profit after tax
Dividend
Retained profit
```

2   Complete the following statements with a suitable word.

    a Assets that are to be kept and used in the business are _____ assets.

    b Assets that are expected to be turned into cash very soon are _____ assets.

    Why is it important to identify the difference between types of asset?

    _____

    _____

    _____

    _____

3   Match the following items with their descriptions.

    a Working capital.   (i)   Statement in which assets equal liabilities.

    b Capital employed.   (ii) Current assets less current liabilities.

    c Depreciation.   (iii) Amount written off the value of a fixed asset.

    d Balance sheet.   (iv) Long-term liabilities and owner's funds.

4   What is the current ratio of a charity with current assets of £240,000 and current liabilities of £400,000?

    _____

    _____

    _____

5   This charity has a stock figure of £120,000 in the balance sheet. What is the quick ratio or acid test?

_____

_____

_____

6   Write down the ratio used to find the profit margin. It is expressed as a percentage (%).

_____

_____

_____

7   Which financial statement do you use to find the figures for the profit margin?

_____

8   What should you do to check if the profit margin is acceptable or a problem?

_____

_____

9   Write down the ratio you would use to find the return on capital employed from company accounts.

Return on capital employed = —————————— × 100

10 How do you work out 'capital employed'?

_____

_____

11 Why is the cash flow forecast a useful aid when measuring business performance?

_____

_____

_____

12 Why is it important to understand the business of the organization when measuring its performance?

_____

_____

_____

Answers to these questions can be found on pages 201–2.

6 Summary

- A profit and loss account measures financial performance over a defined period. From it you can learn what a business has earned (revenue) and what it has spent (operating expenses).

- To arrive at profit before tax, all operating expenses, including interest paid on loans and depreciation, must be included.

- The retained profit is obtained after dividends have been paid to shareholders, if it is for a company. The figure is transferred to the balance sheet and is the surplus money that is re-invested in the business.

- Money and anything that can be turned into money are **assets**.

- Claims against the company are **liabilities**.

- Assets are either:

  - current: they are (or could be) turned into cash fairly quickly;
  - fixed: they are kept and used by the business rather than being turned into cash.

- A balance sheet is a snapshot at a particular time of the business' assets and liabilities balanced against each other. It shows what a business owns (assets) balanced by how these assets are financed (liabilities).

- Non-profit organizations prepare income and expenditure accounts, which are very similar to profit and loss accounts. A surplus is transferred to the accumulated fund in the organization's balance sheet, or to some other specific fund or reserve.

- Financial indicators can be used to measure the business performance of an organization.

- The indicators are usually expressed as ratios or percentages, and provide a guide to performance, particularly if we compare this year with previous years.

- The indicators need to be compared to other companies in the same business or against an 'industry standard' in order to get a true picture of a particular business performance.

- A cash flow forecast will provide helpful additional information about the solvency of an organization because it shows the **expected** performance, which can be compared with what is actually happening.

Session D
Sources of finance

1 Introduction

You've decided that a holiday would do you good. Corfu looks ideal but you've only saved £400 of the £900 cost. What can you do? You might ask the bank for an overdraft if you think you can repay it quickly, or perhaps a personal loan if it's going to take a year or more to pay back.

Organizations have similar problems. Any activity, and particularly any major investment, needs financing. If you work in a large organization your work area probably has a budget for expenditure each year. Perhaps additional money can be asked for in the case of major changes. But where does that money for the budget come from? And does it matter if the need is for the short term, say to cover an increase in credit allowed to continue, or the medium or long term?

In this session we'll look at the various ways in which finance can be obtained, and over what periods of time.

2 Funds available

Identifying sources of funds is the art of the possible. An organization's planning has to take into account how much finance is available and when. Public organizations particularly have money allocated annually; once the budget is spent, no more is available. This often leads to expenditure on projects early in the financial year and cut-backs at the end.

Some organizations have one budget for day-to-day expenditure such as wages and materials. This is a revenue budget. They have a capital budget for longer-term projects.

3 Short-term finance

In the holiday example in the introduction to this session we looked at savings and an overdraft. These are two common sources of short-term finance for organizations as well, although we call 'savings' retained profits. Organizations can also take advantage of trade credit, much as you or I might use the credit period allowed on a credit card to 'fund' our expenditure temporarily.

3.1 Retained profits

We saw earlier that retained profits (or accumulated surpluses in non-profit organizations) are built up through operations and are put into keeping organizations going on a day-to-day basis and in helping them grow. For instance, a manufacturing company may use £200,000 of materials in 2003 and use the profits generated from the sale of the goods manufactured from those materials to buy £250,000 of materials in 2004.

Retained profits are the major source of finance for businesses. One reason for this is that organizations do not have to pay interest or dividends to use retained profits. But, like money you put into a building society to earn interest, if you use it to buy something, you lose interest. Organizations ought to use money in the most effective way, so if they could earn more money investing in a bank deposit or building society account than in a new project, they should not use funds on that project.

Activity 50

5 mins

Organizations often use some money to pay day-to-day expenses such as wages while allowing customers one month's credit. Is this a good use of their money? Why?

_____

_____

I hope you will agree that providing credit is a good use of money because it generates more sales and profits above the cost of providing credit. So financing credit to customers is sensible using cheap retained profits, but would an overdraft be as effective?

3.2 Bank overdraft

Interest usually needs to be paid at high rates on an overdraft, so organizations would not wish to keep an overdraft at a high level for too long. However, overdrafts are useful for fluctuating, short-term needs.

Activity 51 · 5 mins

Pat runs a small chain of food shops and is charged VAT on some of the purchases that she makes for the shops. As she doesn't charge VAT to her customers she finds that she regularly reclaims the VAT that she paid on her purchases from the Customs and Excise Department (C & E). While she is waiting for payment from C & E at the end of each three month period, she often finds that she goes overdrawn at the bank. This overdraft is repaid in full when C & E pay.

Is this a good use of a bank overdraft? Explain your answer.

_____

_____

This is an ideal use of an overdraft because it is quickly repaid by the organization, so it does not have to pay much interest and the overdraft is used for a purpose that pays it back directly.

3.3 Trade credit

Stocks of material and utility bills are regularly financed by trade credit. Your organization is the customer of its various suppliers and they provide you with credit for the same reasons that you allow your customers credit.

Trade credit generally does not cost anything in the way of interest.

4 Medium-term and long-term finance

Organizations often need finance for a longer period than a few months (i.e. the short-term). Money may be needed now to be used up over, say, two years (the medium-term), or over several years (the long-term).

4.1 Retained profits

It should not be a surprise to you to meet retained profits again. You will have short-term, medium-term and long-term saving yourself. You might save up from your earnings for the deposit on a house, for a cruise to celebrate a big anniversary, or for retirement. Many organizations take a similar approach, by noting retained profit.

Activity 52

5 mins

List **two** long-term projects that have been paid for by your organization through retained profits (or surpluses).

_____

_____

You may find it difficult to separate how much is provided from retained profits and how much from other sources in a pool of money for investment. Nevertheless you should have found that retained profits form a major part of the overall investment.

Another important source of finance is borrowing.

4.2 Loans

Sometimes money is not available from retained profits. There may be limited funds in the organization or the money may be tied up already. If this is the situation, and the organization has a promising new project, it may wish to borrow money.

Activity 53

3 mins

Linespar Ltd borrowed £20,000 from the bank for two years at an interest rate linked to market rates but currently quoted at 6 per cent. This is to finance a new project with a return estimated at 12 per cent (before interest on the loan).

Suggest **two** problems which might occur over the two years that could make the new project less attractive.

_____

_____

The return is purely an estimate. If the new project is not as successful as expected, the return may be less than projected. The company is looking for a net 6 per cent return, being the return on the new project less the interest charge, so it has little room for manoeuvre before it starts to make a loss.

In addition, the interest rate on the loan is linked to market rates and any changes in these could increase or decrease the profit from the new project.

All activities have some risk attached, but potential problems should be identified and allowed for. The new project described above is likely to be more viable if financed through retained profits.

Is funding through share capital different?

4.3 Share capital

By purchasing shares, shareholders buy a financial interest in the organization. In return for their investment they may have voting rights and will expect part of the profits – dividends – in proportion to their shareholding.

Companies can raise capital through different kinds of share capital. Shareholders expect some income from their investment by way of dividends so, again, the expected return is important for any activity to be financed by shares.

Shares, or equity, finance is usually kept for very long-term investments because it is far more difficult to repay them than to pay back loans. In addition, public companies particularly are concerned to maintain investor confidence and maintain a good share price. They must make the best use of the finance.

Activity 54

What would be the consequence for a company which financed a four-year project by shares, after which time the investment had been paid back two-fold?

_____

_____

_____

I hope you will agree that the company would have surplus money. Unless it could find another profitable source of investment for the cash it would only be able to invest it in banks, building societies, government and company investments. Usually this would provide a lower return than projects in the course of trade and might not pay the dividends that investors expected.

4.4 Grants

Many non-profit organizations, like charities and some others in the public sector, are financed by grants. These are funds which need not be paid back, generally providing certain conditions are fulfilled. However, to get the grants, organizations need to apply and convince the grant provider that the money is to be used appropriately. For instance, a branch of Age Concern might receive a grant of 50 per cent of the cost of a day centre if:

- the local branch raised the other 50 per cent itself;
- the project would meet the needs of, say, 25 people a day;
- the day-to-day running of the project would be self-financing;
- certain management and operational criteria are met.

Activity 55

Suppose your organization agreed to provide a grant for a social club and provide grounds for sports. Suggest two ways in which the day-to-day running of the club could be self-financing.

_____

_____

Profits from the sale of food and drink are a common source of finance for social clubs. You might also have suggested membership fees, subscriptions, profits from dinner dances and other functions.

5 Flexible financing

Your organization may be short of funds but may need, say, a couple of additional vans to enable service staff to travel to customers and generate income from essential maintenance work.

The bank may not wish to lend any more to the organization and such investments are not appropriate for share issues and grants. Leasing and hire purchase offer the answer. The vans can be paid for at the same time as they are being used to earn money. After a period of time the organization may or may not own the vans but it will certainly have use of them.

Self-assessment 4

15 mins

1   a Name two types of short-term finance.

_____

_____

b Name two types of long-term finance.

_____

_____

2   Briefly explain why the interest rate charged on borrowing is important when deciding whether to finance a new project in this way.

_____

_____

3   Briefly explain when leasing may be a useful source of finance.

_____

_____

4   What makes retained profits a popular source of finance?

_____

5   Homes for the Homeless is a charity which buys old houses, renovates them and provides them at a low rent for homeless families. Suggest how the charity would finance its work.

_____

_____

_____

Answers to these questions can be found on pages 202–3.

6 Summary

- Organizations require finance even if it is repaid quickly. Some may require short-term finance and some finance for the medium or longer term.

- Short-term finance is used to meet day-to-day needs and can be supplied from retained profits, bank overdrafts and trade credit.

- Medium-term and long-term finance is provided from retained profits, share capital, loans and, generally in non-profit organizations, grants.

- If funds are not easily available, hire purchase or leases can be used if equipment and machinery can pay for regular payments from its operation.

- The cost of finance is important. The greater the cost of the finance, the greater the return needed from activities to meet the financing cost. Retained profits are generated from operations and are cheap. Ideally, organizations would wish to earn more from the use of retained profits than would be gained from putting the money into a bank deposit or building society account.

Session E
The economic environment

■ 1 Introduction

The effects of the economic policies of governments and, increasingly, of multinational corporations may seem remote from everyday life. But:

- a government decision to reduce the subsidy paid to a particular industry may show in the closure of facilities such as farms, mines and factories with direct loss of jobs;
- a decision to provide start-up finance may, conversely, lead to the creation of new facilities by overseas companies and the creation of employment in the short or long term;
- the decision of a multinational concern to relocate production facilities from, say, Scotland to China in pursuit – perhaps – of cheaper labour and lower safety, health and welfare standards will have direct local impact on employment and morale in the community.

The abolition of individual farms and their forcible grouping into collectives under the communist regime in Russia contributed to famine in the 1930s.

Conversely, in the USA President Roosevelt was tackling the consequences of previous right-wing policies which had little concern for what happened to individuals, and might have led to the rise of socialism in America – the bastion of free enterprise.

Whereas it was once common for employees to spend the whole of their working lives with one local employer, generation succeeding generation, this pattern is now very much the exception, even in formerly safe employment in banks, insurance companies, public utilities (electricity, gas, water, telecommunications) and railways.

If you look at the jobs which members of your own family have done since the end of World War Two (1939–1945), the changing pattern will almost certainly become apparent.

Some factors which directly affect people's everyday working lives are beyond the direct control of man. Examples include climate and weather, and natural disasters such as flooding, earthquakes and plagues (whether of locusts or the bubonic plague which killed millions of Europeans in the Middle Ages).

In the early twentieth century much of the stock of grapevines in France was wiped out by the phyloxera virus. Wine making, of colossal economic importance and significance to national morale, was affected disastrously. It was eventually rescued by the importation of resistant strains from California – where they had been taken by economic migrants in the previous century.

Economic policies carried to either extreme of the political spectrum can produce profound and often disastrous consequences for organizations and the individuals who work for them.

The UK has never swung to either end of the political spectrum, but the protectionist Corn Laws of the 1830s and 1840s were a contributory factor to famine in Ireland. The result was a mass migration of people to America, and the memory of the famine still influences political attitudes in the twenty-first century, well over 150 years later.

All these issues raise moral, ethical, financial and economic questions to which there are seldom clear cut answers. The following activity illustrates the complexities involved.

Activity 56 · 8 mins

You have come across a headline in the press that says carpets sold through a major chain of stores in the UK are being produced by child labour (from the age of six upwards) in sweatshops in central Asia. Child workers are preferred to adults because their small hands are claimed to be ideal for tying the tiny knots which give the carpets their undoubted quality. The children are paid a pittance by UK standards. The newspaper reports that there are fears about the long-term effects on the children's eyesight, and there is a risk of their developing arthritis in their fingers.

It would be quite practical for the carpets to be produced by means of power looms in the UK or Belgium. This would provide more employment in those countries, reduce the price to buyers and possibly generate more sales for the retailer. The machine-made carpets would still be of high quality, but would not match the hand-made originals.

However, there would be no chance of alternative employment for the children in Asia and there is no state schooling available to them.

1   Think about this scenario for a while and then suggest at least three reasons which the Asian sweatshop owners might advance for keeping production where it is.

_____

_____

_____

2   In one sentence, give your opinion of what would be the correct course of action. Do not exceed the time allotted to this activity.

_____

_____

_____

_____

The sweatshop owners might argue that:

- there is nothing else for the children to do;
- they are learning a skilled trade;
- their parents are dependent on their income;
- the cost of living is much lower, so they do not need European levels of pay;
- if they can't make carpets they will starve – so there is little point in worrying about their long-term health;
- the quality which their small fingers produce is what the discerning customer wants and is prepared to pay for;
- if sweatshops close, the children together with their immediate families and all the suppliers involved in the trade will suffer hardships unimaginable in a country which has state welfare provision;
- the land around the sweatshops is stony, barren and unsuited to growing crops – but the sheep whose wool is used can make do on the poor pasture which it offers.

The familiar paisley pattern associated with the Scottish town of Paisley and used in shawls, neckties, headscarves and many other goods is in fact an Eastern pattern which the ingenious manufacturers found ways of mass-producing. This created employment in Scotland, but deprived the Eastern craftsmen of at least a part of their market. So there were winners and losers in this real example.

You may have thought of other reasons. There will be as many one sentence views of what is the correct solution as there are readers of this workbook. For example, employing the children's parents instead, which would result in only a small increase in costs and actually no reduction in quality. As customers become aware of the conditions in which goods are produced, they may become less willing to buy them.

This case has no solution at a price **willingly affordable** to all parties. Inevitably there will be winners and losers whatever decision the retailer comes to.

The purpose of this activity was to stress the complexity of economic decision making and the moral and ethical dimensions which such decisions entail.

2 How economics affects everyone

We will now look at how some of the matters described in the last section may have affected you personally.

Activity 57

2 mins

Think about your own working situation and the influence, for good or ill, that governments, multinationals and natural occurrences have had on it. Describe each influencing factor in the first column, then explain in what way it was an influence for good or ill. You may find that some of the factors have both good and bad influences.

Factor	Influence for good	Influence for ill
Government decision:		
Decision by multinational company:		
Natural occurrence:		

Your experiences will differ widely, but it is very likely that you have been affected by at least one of the influences listed, whatever your job. For example:

It is said that if you ask three economists in a room to recommend a solution to a problem, they will come up with at least four answers. Having begun to see how difficult the choices are, you may decide that this isn't perhaps so surprising.

- overseas companies have established factories here as the result of government policy, especially policy involving development grants in areas perceived as economically deprived;
- some of these companies have gone elsewhere again, as soon as the benefits to them have worn off or new incentives have been offered elsewhere; this has happened in the UK under both Conservative and Labour Governments;
- policies such as privatization have led to radical changes in employment patterns for millions of people in such industries as mining, transport, public utilities and naval dockyards;
- anyone involved in food manufacturing will have been affected at some time by bumper harvests or by total crop failures caused by bad weather or disease;
- policies aimed at improving the health, safety and working conditions of people in Western Europe have had the effect of driving up the costs of employment here compared with developing countries or even with those countries in Eastern Europe which are hoping to join the European Union (EU);
- changes in taxation policy can influence the ability of people to support charities and reduce the value of the contributions which they make.

These opening sections have invited you to think about the consequences of what is often called macroeconomics – a study of economics that looks at the 'big picture' of world economics. It tries to explain how the human influences of politics, global business decisions, trends in population numbers and consumption interact with influences largely outside the control of man (such as the climate) to build up the picture which the observer can see in total – a bit like a completed jigsaw with all its pieces in place.

It can include situations as diverse as that of young carpet weavers in Central Asia and your own situation. The aim has been to get you to think in terms of the ethical dimension of trade, as well as the objective dimension which can be measured in terms of profit and loss accounts and balance sheet figures.

Joseph de Maistre, a French philosopher who lived from 1753 to 1821 said: 'Each country has the government it deserves'.

In general the economic decisions taken by elected governments reflect the attitudes of the voters who have elected them. These are a mixture of:

- rational decisions arrived at through practical thought processes; and
- emotional decisions which come from the heart.

The electorate has, over time, the power to influence policy. That is why it is important for all the members of an electorate to take an interest in the economic policies which their government pursues. They will then be in a position to make an informed choice about what general direction is acceptable in policy-making.

3 Factors of production

Factors of production are the three elements which any organization must combine in varying amounts to produce any product or service. No organization, whatever its purpose, can operate without utilizing these three factors. One of the factors is land – for example, the land on which an office factory, hospital or distribution depot is situated. The other two factors are capital and labour.

The term 'capital' is used to refer to a whole range of physical assets – from a power station to a computer. For convenience such assets are usually expressed in terms of what they would cost to buy or replace. However, money of itself cannot produce goods or services. It has to be used to buy a physical asset – a machine, a vehicle, a piece of computer software, before it can combine with land and labour to produce goods and services.

Activity 58 · 3 mins

Below is a list of fifteen items used in the production of a good or service. Allocate each of them to one of the three factors of production. You should finish up with five items under each factor.

development site delivery vehicle agricultural field computer

receptionist economist combine harvester shop worker

managing director garage forecourt video camera car park

power station riverside wharf itinerant fruit picker

Land	Capital	Labour

You will find an answer to this activity on page 207.

You may have needed to think fairly hard about some of the items where there may be a blurring between capital and land. For example:

- a power station is definitely capital, but the **site** on which it stands is land;
- a garage forecourt is **land** but equipment such as pumps and the overhead canopy are **capital**.

It is perhaps less surprising that all the people listed are labour. But it might be a chastening experience for economists to be listed alongside itinerant fruit pickers. To an economist, both are labour – though one category is no doubt paid much more than the other!

Does all this really matter other than to economists? Well yes it does, both to you and your organization, as you will see from the following activities.

3.1 The pressure to become least cost producer

One of the stated aims of many organizations nowadays is to be the least cost producer in their field, i.e. the producer who produces a product or service at the lowest possible cost in terms of land, capital and labour. This is vital to many commercial companies driven by pressure from supermarket buyers or overseas competition, but it is also true of many other organizations, not only those which are commercial or profit-driven. For example, organizations such as hospitals, schools, local authorities and the courts are required to operate within tight budgets and must look constantly to control their costs.

The way organizations most frequently seek to reduce costs is by:

- replacing one factor of production with a cheaper one, say replacing skilled workers with unskilled ones;
- reducing the cost of an individual factor, such as land – say by moving offices from London to a city where office rents are lower.

There are many ways of reducing costs, as the next activity will demonstrate.

Activity 59 · 5 mins

The Landor company manufactures children's clothes. It sells exclusively to high street retailers who market them under their own brands. Landor is coming under increasing pressure to reduce its prices because its three largest customers are all keen to improve their profit margins.

Landor prides itself on a high quality, machine-made but hand-embroidered product manufactured from soft, durable fabric. The customers insist that the fabric should not be downgraded. All staff are paid the agreed union rates for their work and there is one team leader to every eight staff. The present machinery is running at an average 65% of maximum throughput annually.

Suggest four ways in which Landor could move towards being a least cost producer by changing the costs of its **capital** and **labour** factors of production and the proportions in which they use them.

For practical purposes, there is nothing that they can do about their location in the short term, so the cost of their **land** is fixed.

You may have considered the following options:

Capital

- changing to machine embroidery from hand-sewn embroidery, to reduce the labour cost;
- installing faster machines, or speeding up existing ones, so that fewer operators can process the same output through fewer machines;
- closing approximately 35% of its machines and transferring their production to the remaining 65%. If this were practicable, it would then be running the remaining machines at nearer 100% capacity, resulting in much more efficiency and fewer people;
- finding other work to fill the machines, so that their overheads can be spread over a larger number of items. At present, they have up to 35% spare capacity.

Labour

- switching production to a country where payment rates are lower;
- reducing the level of supervision from 1:8 operators to 1:10 or even 1:12;
- introducing piece work or bonus schemes which offer operators the chance to increase earnings through increased output per worker.

This very simple example shows clearly how important the management of factors of production can be to any organization.

This activity was concerned with capital and labour, so what about the third factor of production, **land**? The UK is one of the most densely populated countries in Europe – less than **half** the size of France, but with a similar population (approaching 60 million in 2002). The mountainous areas of Wales, Scotland, the north of England and Northern Ireland are unsuitable for large towns and are remote from potential markets, increasing the pressure on lower lying areas in all four countries.

It is frequently said that land is the scarcest economic resource because you can't make any more of it. But is this true?

This case illustrates in simple terms what has been happening to so many industries in the UK and elsewhere over the past 50 years. Machinery has become faster and more able to imitate skilled human work. Faster distribution systems world-wide have enabled organizations to look for cheaper labour away from the developed world and to buy good products anywhere on earth.

Activity 60 · 2 mins

Can you think of one or two examples in Europe of countries which have made more land – other than by seizing someone else's!

1 _____

_____

2 _____

_____

Large-scale examples include:

- the polder land of The Netherlands (an even more densely populated country than the UK), where vast tracts of land have been reclaimed from the North Sea and turned into productive farmland;
- the fen country in the English counties of Lincolnshire, Bedfordshire, Norfolk and Cambridgeshire, where similar drainage works changed the romantic – but unproductive – areas of low lying misty marshland into prime agricultural land;
- similar areas of Romney Marsh in Kent and East Sussex which were also once under the sea.

Though these and other examples are very significant, they represent a small proportion of the total land of each country and are very much exceptions to the rule.

The once important, thriving town of Dunwich in Norfolk has disappeared beneath the North Sea, as have whole areas of the Holderness area of East Yorkshire.

Gloomy predictions about climatic change suggest that the North Sea will, in any case, take back equivalent areas in the foreseeable future. Coastal erosion has been wearing away areas around the UK's long coastline for centuries, sometimes flooding whole towns.

So, while the opportunities to make more land are limited, you can put what you have to different uses:

Billy Butlin realized that, following World War One (1914–1918), there were many surplus army camps, some of them sited in potential holiday locations, such as Skegness. On the basis of that observation, he acquired land cheaply and changed its purpose from **military** camp to **holiday** camp. He thus founded the business which still bears his name, has provided holidays for millions of people, and was still the largest employer in Skegness in 2002.

The Gulf State of Dubai is sparsely populated and has abundant land, most of it unusable for most purposes because of the extreme temperatures and desert conditions. However; Dubai is currently a major supplier of oil. It also has an international airport used as a stopover for long-distance flights.

The ruling family decided to turn much of the coastal land into leisure facilities to attract visitors from all over the world. With abundant oil revenues, they could afford to build (and run) air-conditioned hotels, irrigate the desert and create golf courses, race courses and leisure facilities using the sea.

They are looking long-term. The oil will eventually run out, so their intention is to create an alternative economy, based on leisure, sales of duty-free goods, tourism and the international airport.

Both these case studies show how enterprising people can make good alternative use of land, even if they cannot create it.

▣ 4 Raw materials

You will have noticed that the three factors of production do not include the raw materials used by organizations.

This is because raw materials are actually consumed and must be replaced continuously if the work is to continue. Take a corned beef plant in Argentina, for instance, tinplate, cattle, corn and seasonings go in one end of the factory and tins of corned beef come out the other end.

If you want more corned beef, you must put in more of each raw material, but the factors of production, i.e. the land on which the buildings stand, the factory equipment and the staff, are all still there ready to process the next batch.

So, while the various factors of production are constant items in the production process, raw materials are consumed and must be provided continuously if the process is to be sustained. The materials vary from one organization to another, but every organization has them.

Activity 61 · 8 mins

Look at the different types of organization listed in the table below, then enter the items from the following list into the appropriate columns. All the items are either factors of production or raw materials.

One answer has been inserted under each organization as an example of what is required.

computerized switchboard	shop assistant	rented garage	football pitch
travelling oven	car park	office space	rented shop
sub editor	X ray machine	print room	customer care assistant
standard letters	goalkeeper	high-speed press	flour and water
goods delivery notes	computer	gymnasium	surgeon
dressings	entrepreneur	practice balls	ink

Organization	Land	Capital	Labour	Raw materials
Hospital	car park			
Call centre				standard letters
Internet marketing firm		computer		
Take-away pizza shop			shop assistant	
Newspaper		high-speed press		
Football club	football pitch			

Studies in the years 2000 and 2001 have shown that the supposed paperless office of the computer age is actually consuming **more** paper – the raw material of commercial life. Vast numbers of emails, management information, advertising materials, etc. are sent electronically, but subsequently printed out.

The answers can be found on page 208. There may be one or two items which you have assigned differently, but most will square with the model provided.

The last activity asked you to think about some of the important factors of production, showing that even the highest paid surgeon or soccer superstar is 'labour' in economic terms.

The next activity brings together many of the points that have been covered under factors of production and raw materials.

Activity 62

Think about the activities of your own organization and list the principal factors of production and raw materials used:

- in your own area of responsibility;
- for your total site or the organization generally.

For many organizations, this could produce a very long list, so please use your discretion to prioritize them and list only the top five or so in each category.

	Land	Capital	Labour	Raw materials
Your area of responsibility				
Your site or organization generally				

4.1 Renewable and non-renewable resources

Renewable resources

Renewable resources are raw materials which can reproduce themselves, given suitable conditions – such as food or fuel crops, trees, animals and fish. Power from wind, tides and the flow of rivers are also renewable, as is solar power captured directly from the sun.

However, as a result of the way the world has been 'managed' for many years now, even renewable resources are under threat or have already been reduced to dangerously low levels. For example:

Economics is frequently called the gloomy science, at least in part because it forces people to face issues that they hope will go away if ignored. But the issues won't, even if the resources do.

- the North American buffalo was all but made extinct by unfettered hunting in the nineteenth century;
- stocks of fish in the oceans are under serious threat;
- timber has been plundered to such an extent from the rain forests of South America and South East Asia that another seemingly limitless resource could be threatened;
- the desertification of areas in several continents which could once grow food crops, another renewable resource is proceeding at an alarming rate.

In the case study about Dubai, reference was made to the oil – on which the state's wealth rests – eventually running out. Many or the world's resources are in this category. That simple fact has a profound influence on economic policies and the way in which all organizations must manage their affairs.

Non-renewable resources

Non-renewable resources are in an even more dire situation. These are resources that do not reproduce themselves, such as coal, oil and natural gas – the very sources of power which literally drove the industrial revolution which began in the eighteenth century.

Many of these resources are running down or having to be extracted from increasingly remote and expensive sites.

No wonder that economics is often called the 'gloomy science'! However, there is no way of avoiding the consequences of these macroeconomic factors; they affect everyone sooner or later, if only because the prices of all the items concerned – or products containing them – will be driven relentlessly upwards.

For example, dwindling fish stocks have led to steep price increases for fish and chips. As cod, plaice and haddock become scarcer, their price increases to reflect their scarcity and the increased costs of landing them from more remote fisheries.

5 The price mechanism

Henry Ford said that the ideal product:

'costs a dime (10 cents) sells for a dollar **and** every home must have one'.

He was right when he said it – and just as right 100 years or more later.

Each of the factors of production has a price, as do the raw materials which each organization uses.

■ In simple terms, the more abundant the factor or material, the less it will cost. The scarcer it becomes, the more expensive it becomes.
■ If there is no market for it, i.e. if no one wants it, then scarcity will have little or no effect on price. For example, if fur-bearing animals are scarce, but people give up wearing fur for ethical reasons, then the price of fur will not be high.

Let's look at the price mechanism in relation to each factor of production.

5.1 Land

The price of land varies according to its scarcity.

Skyscrapers were built in American cities because it seemed that every business must be in Manhattan or a particular, limited area of Chicago – so the only way was up.

If you've ever flown over the UK at night, the contrast between brilliantly lit conurbations like London, Birmingham, Manchester and Glasgow and the darkness of rural counties like Shropshire, Cumbria and Lincolnshire is vividly apparent.

Much earlier, many British and European towns acquired the typically narrow shop fronts onto the high street which they still exhibit today. It was essential to display your wares in a particular area of the town, so property values increased and it was cheaper to have long, narrow shops than wide, shallow ones. Local tax policies also encouraged this approach.

Agricultural land varies in price according to what you can do with it. Prime arable land, found in the eastern counties of England, will grow high-value crops like bread-making wheat. It costs substantially more than hill pasture in Wales which is suitable only for cattle or sheep farming and produces lower returns per acre.

In times of agricultural depression, the price of farmland of all types will tend to fall. Sometimes farmers will build up their holdings in anticipation of a later recovery, just as dealers will buy stocks and shares when they believe them to have bottomed out.

The UK has particularly expensive land in world terms because of its high population density and the concentration of people and business activity in a few areas.

The price of housing, office space and industrial land in the conurbations simply reflects competition between buyers of land who must live or operate in those areas.

Other places where land prices are always high and rising include Hong Kong, Singapore and Monaco. All are small places, with little or no chance of expanding.

Activity 63

10 mins

Think about your own organization and any effect which land prices have had on its present location. For example, has it always been where it is now, or has it relocated from a city centre site to an industrial estate, or to offices in a satellite town?

Has it sold a prime site in a city centre for development and used the cash generated to fund the move to cheaper premises in terms of rent and rates?

There are any number of possibilities, but so many organizations have relocated because of increasing land prices, that yours may well have been affected. List any land/price related issues which you can identify.

_____

_____

_____

_____

5.2 Capital

As you have seen, the definition of capital takes in massive items such as agricultural machinery, power stations and operating theatres through to small items such as computers and other office equipment.

The price of some equipment, particularly in data processing, has moved downwards over many years, and this is partly why so many office-based jobs are now dependent upon it – or have been replaced by it.

The price of many items of machinery has increased because of the safety features which are legally required by governments.

The cost of buses is increased by the requirement to provide access for the disabled, a factor which may produce increased income through disabled people being able to use the vehicles.

The price of some capital items increases because they are built from materials which are themselves scarce or expensive to manufacture, such as aluminium and titanium used in aircraft construction.

5.3 Labour

Wages, salaries, piece-work rates, commissions, royalties and fees are all ways of expressing the price of labour. You may be able to think of others.

The price of labour is affected by its scarcity or abundance in the same way as the price of the other factors of production.

The wages of agricultural labourers increased substantially in the Middle Ages after the Black Death wiped out a large percentage of all such workers in a few terrible years.

If you think back to the children in Activity 1, they are in plentiful supply and so can demand only minimal wages. Even though their work is skilled, the skills they possess can be readily taught to other children. In the absence of any regulation of child labour, there is no reason in **economic** terms why they should be paid any more in an economy where wages are generally low and unemployment typically high.

In the UK, the indigenous population is stable and there are strict rules about what work children can undertake. There is also strict minimum wage legislation which an employer cannot breach, even if employees are prepared to work for less. Unlike in poorer countries, there are also 'on costs' which increase the price of labour. These are the costs that are over and above the direct costs of wages or salary, and it is worth identifying them.

Activity 64

2 mins

List the typical on costs which an employer must bear in addition to the direct price which an employee charges for his or her labour.

_____

_____

_____

_____

_____

The answer can be found on page 208.

The price of labour is more sensitive a subject than that of capital or land because even the highest paid individuals tend to believe that they are worth **at least** what they receive now – if not more. How often have you heard a footballer, a show business personality, the chairman of a public company or a politician propose taking a pay cut, however highly they are paid? Have **you** ever believed you were overpaid for what you were doing and asked the organization you worked for to give you a pay cut?

Rationally, if the price of labour increases beyond what an employer is prepared to pay, then that employer will try either to:

> One American multinational company has put forward the idea of a 'floating factory' which can sail from port to port in pursuit of the optimum combination of an able workforce willing to work for the lowest wages. This graphic concept, though it may never become reality, shows just how companies think in the twenty-first century.

■ find someone else prepared to work for less, possibly in another country, as increasing numbers of employers are doing; or

■ replace labour with capital – bigger, faster machinery, or automatic systems which can duplicate at least some of the tasks which human beings typically undertake.

Human resources have a maximum affordable price, just like any other factor of production. It is a hard fact of economic life.

5.4 The price mechanism and competition

The combined prices of all the factors of production and the costs of raw materials all feed through into the price which producers charge to the eventual users of their products.

In 'mixed' or 'free market' economies, such as those in the UK and Western Europe, the consumer has a choice as to:

■ who to buy a product or service from;
■ whether to buy it at all.

For example, if you are thinking about using a mobile phone, you can choose from a wide range of companies, all of whom claim to be the best. **You** can decide which is the best for you, or you can choose not to have a mobile phone at all.

If you believe electricity is too expensive, or you don't like your present supplier, you can change supplier or move to natural or bottled gas, oil, coal, wood fires – according to your needs and desires. You are not stuck with a particular supplier who can tell you to take it or leave it if you complain. You don't even need a good reason to change, you can do so on a whim.

Activity 65 · 2 mins

Can you think of one commodity in the UK which:

■ is essential to life, i.e. we should die rapidly if deprived of it;
■ is available from only one supplier in any given area of the country;
■ is provided by a private, profit-making organization.

_____

_____

_____

_____

_____

Command economy
Under a state-directed or 'command' economy, such as those of the former USSR and the People's Republic of China under communism, the State acquired the means of:

■ production;
■ distribution;
■ exchange (in effect, banking).

The state exercised a monopoly over every aspect of people's lives for many years. In the latter part of the twentieth century, both these huge countries have moved towards a mixed economy.

The answer can be found on pages 208–9. You may have thought of a different example. The answer given touches on the subject of monopoly, which will be expanded on shortly.

There are any number of choices available in a mixed economy for the basic human needs of food, shelter and clothing. For example:

■ if you own some land, you can grow at least some of your food for yourself – and keep some chickens as well;
■ you can buy or rent a house, or find a room in someone else's house if you prefer. If you do decide to buy, then there are many mortgage options available;
■ for clothing, again, there are countless shops, mail order and Internet businesses from whom you can buy. Or you can buy materials such as wool, cotton and silk and make at least some of them for yourself.

It is competition between organizations which prevents them from charging what they please and maximizing their profits at your expense.

5.5 Monopoly

But what would happen if there should be only **one** supplier, or if a number of large suppliers get together and agree to charge the same price? From their point of view, that makes everything much simpler:

■ they can plan ahead on the basis of known prices and a guaranteed market share;
■ they need have no fear of being undercut by a rival;
■ they can fix the price to produce whatever return they like on the factors of production which they use, and maximize their profit if they so desire;
■ they really can tell people to take it or leave it if they complain about their goods, services or prices.

Monopoly prevents the price mechanism from working. It is outlawed or severely constrained in the UK, as described in the answer to Activity 64.

The former state monopolies which were privatized in the late twentieth century are all regulated by independent bodies. For example, in the USA, there has also been legislation to eliminate or minimize the effects of private monopolies through the anti-trust laws. These attempt to prevent large private businesses getting together and rigging the market.

Though monopoly seems a most attractive condition if you are a supplier, it is harder to sustain than many hopeful monopolists have thought. This piece of economists' wisdom explains one of the basic flaws with all monopolies:

> 'the fortunate monopolist can charge what price he chooses, but if he cannot sell enough, he doesn't gain, he loses'.

The sad facts of life from the monopolist's point of view are that:

- competition will always be attracted to move in on a monopoly, tempted by the artificially high profit margins it has generated;
- there are very few products for which consumers cannot find a substitute;
- consumers resent monopolistic practices and, unless they are enforced by law (as under communist regimes), will try hard to find ways of undermining them.

A manufacturer had patented a process for making speciality papers. It was the only UK manufacturer for a product which many offices had to have. It charged accordingly and for some years made profits which far exceeded what its costs of production would justify.

Overseas manufacturers could not breach the patent but, seeing a profitable market, developed alternative products. Though technically not as good, they did the job adequately at a substantially lower price and still yielded an acceptable return on their substantial investment. Resentful customers moved in significant numbers to the alternative suppliers and their substantially cheaper new materials.

The monopolist's sales fell and it was forced eventually to cut prices. By that time the highly specialist equipment it had installed was growing old and needed replacement at a cost that was hard to justify in the changed market conditions.

Monopoly, like so many features of economic life which seem permanent, is actually more often a temporary feature. Ultimately, the price mechanism which adjusts demand to supply will have its way, unless the monopoly is sustained by laws or by physical force.

5.6 Subsidy

Subsidies are another mechanism which can distort the price mechanism. Governments through the ages have used them for a wide range of purposes. For example, the European Union (EU) has subsidized agricultural products throughout its existence.

Very often, subsidies have been used for benevolent purposes, for example, to ensure that the poorer people in a country can afford the basic necessities of life, say by:

- subsidizing the price of bread or other staple foodstuffs;
- providing low cost housing;
- providing cheaper heating to people vulnerable to cold, typically older people in a cold climate.

Under subsidized pricing:

- the consumer does not pay the full market price for the product or service;
- the producer receives the difference between the subsidized price and the market price from a third party, typically the government.

As an illustration of subsidy at work, imagine that the market price of bread equates to 75 pence per standard 800 gram loaf, but the government decides that the maximum which a defined group of people can afford is 55 pence per loaf. Then the government will pay the balance of 20 pence per loaf to the producer out of its general taxation revenues.

The USA, the avowed home of free enterprise and the market economy, actually provides heavy subsidies to its farmers to make them competitive with imported food. Because the US economy is so huge, this has the effect of distorting the whole world economy.

You might think this is a proper use of subsidy, provided that the wealthier members of society agree to provide the funds which the government requires to pay the difference. But it distorts the normal price mechanism – and subsidies can be used for less ethical purposes, particularly to protect local industries (such as farming and steel production) from overseas competition, perhaps from developing countries where the costs of the factors of production are lower.

In 2002 the collapse of a number of media companies in the UK and Europe threatened the future of some of the most famous football clubs in countries such as Germany, Spain, Italy and the UK.

For years, teams have depended on TV income for a major part of their income. Much of that income has been used to pay wages to players, sometimes of millions of pounds (or euros) per annum. Meanwhile, the number of spectators able and willing to attend matches has fallen and matches have been scheduled to suit the TV companies rather than the fans.

By 2002 TV advertising revenues were falling, pay-to-view channels had found that the majority of potential viewers would **not** pay to watch most matches – and so the incomes of the broadcasters fell dramatically.

TV revenues had in effect subsidized businesses, most of which were not operating in anything like a commercial fashion. A large percentage of that subsidy went in labour cost – players' wages – and straight out of the game. The huge revenues from the years of plenty largely disappeared, and insufficient reserves (of money, not players) were created for the lean years which might follow when the TV companies offer smaller deals to reflect their smaller revenues.

Had the clubs operated under normal price mechanisms over the good years, their finances would almost certainly be in more reasonable shape. Their wages bills would certainly be more affordable.

This example of a subsidy provided by commercial organizations shows how much it can distort things and encourage the recipients to live in a fool's paradise. There could be no philanthropic purpose for subsidizing the life styles of football players. So, as soon as the expected revenues for the TV companies did not materialize, their own future was threatened and they pulled the plug.

Football is not the only sport subsidized by TV. So why have the hard-headed TV moguls been prepared to provide such huge subsidies? Basically because of their need to fill their schedules. The cost of producing dramatized programmes would far outweigh the costs of televising sport such as snooker, darts, athletics – or even Formula 1 racing.

In Germany, there was a suggestion that the federal government should effectively subsidize the clubs affected. Given that four million German people were unemployed in 2002, the idea did not prove universally popular. Most of them would earn less in a lifetime than many football players are paid in one year – and many Germans have no interest in football.

This look at subsidies began by discussing their use to help poorer people. It widened into their use to protect activities like farming or steel production which a country believes is vital to protect for strategic or political reasons. However desirable that may be, the use of subsidies always distorts the working of the price mechanism which is at the heart of capitalism and mixed economies such as that of the UK.

The football case study shows that subsidies also appear in surprising places. Wherever they crop up, they distort the working of the price mechanism – which in the long term will create problems of one kind or another.

The next activity will ask you to look at the factors of price, competition and subsidy as they affect your own organization.

Activity 66 ·

15 mins

Please identify for your own organization:

In Session F we will examine the EU's use of subsidies to agriculture. These consume a high percentage of its total budget and are a constant cause of debate among the EU's institutions, and of friction with other countries, which claim that their food products are penalized or even excluded from fair competition in world markets.

■ who your chief direct competitors are. If you work for an organization such as the National Health Service, you can still be in competition with private sector or overseas providers – there are surprisingly few organizations which have no competition at all.

■ how you believe that your prices compare with those of your direct competitors. This may be more or less easy to discover, according to what your organization does, and it may be necessary for you simply to state your impression of the position.

■ any indirect competition you know of. For example, can people change from your product to another, in the same way as they can swap from electricity to gas, from tube trains to buses or from reading papers to listening to radio news?

■ any subsidies involved which affect your organization. Many organizations will not have any, but the football case study shows that subsidies can turn up in unexpected places.

_____

_____

_____

_____

_____

So far in this session we have looked at:

■ the factors of production;
■ their prices;
■ the price mechanism, which normally keeps supply and demand in balance;
■ issues of subsidized pricing and monopolies – public or private – which distort it.

These economic concepts are fundamental to understanding all economic issues within your own organization and beyond it. Keeping them in mind will help you understand all the larger issues which will be looked at in the remainder of this session and in Session F.

6 The economic levers which governments use

Governments throughout the world try to control the remorseless interplay of supply and demand with varying degrees of success.

Modern governments seem obsessed with economics, but in reality they have far less power than they would like to have.

- They cannot influence natural phenomena which lead to good or bad harvests or make mines and oil fields unworkable.
- They frequently do not understand the methods and the technology employed by multinational companies in pursuing their own independent aims.
- They are in office typically for four or five years and always have an eye to the next election. Many of the economic trends they are endeavouring to influence have much longer cycles.
- Modern developed world economies are so complex, so inter-related, so dependent on energy and so prone to change that it is impossible for anyone to predict what will happen with any degree of accuracy.

Fiscal and monetary policies are often referred to as 'economic levers' which the Government can use to move the UK's enormous economy in the direction it wants it to go. Changes in taxation policy or interest rates bear on the economy in the same way as a physical lever is used to move a heavy weight. The longer the lever, the greater its potential effect on the weight being moved. So, the greater the movement in tax or interest rates up or down, the greater the potential effect on people's spending and saving decisions.

6.1 Fiscal policy

The term 'fiscal policy' refers to the taxes which governments impose to raise money for spending on defence, health, education, social services and other provisions (such as EU member governments' contribution to centralized EU expenditure).

There are basically two types of taxation:

- direct (progressive) taxation;
- indirect (regressive) taxation.

Direct taxation

This is taxation which increases as the income or wealth of individuals or organizations increases. It is frequently called **progressive taxation** – the more you earn, the more you pay.

Activity 67

2 mins

Name two or three direct taxes which are raised by the UK government.

_____

_____

_____

_____

You almost certainly named income tax for individuals and corporation tax for companies, which rise as income rises. In the case of individuals, different rates of tax are applied to different bands of income and so take some account of individuals' ability to pay.

If you have no income, you pay nothing; if your income is relatively high, you pay tax at a higher rate in the pound on the higher part of your taxable income.

National Insurance Contributions (NICs), paid by individuals and employers, are also a form of direct taxation. They again rise as income rises, but in their case only until a fixed upper limit is reached. Stamp duty (paid on property and other capital transactions) and inheritance tax are also forms of direct, progressive taxation.

By increasing or reducing rates of direct taxation, governments can control how much of their earnings individuals and organizations actually keep. This will affect countless decisions on expenditure, which in turn affects the level of economic activity.

Indirect taxation

Indirect taxation takes no account of people's ability to pay and is related to the value of the goods or services which they consume. It is often called 'regressive' tax, because it bears most heavily on individuals with the lowest incomes.

> It is worth remembering that governments by and large have no money of their own. They can only spend what the electorate is prepared to allow them to take in the form of taxes (direct and indirect). When they announce increased spending plans, they are spending the electorate's money and not their own.

For example, the council tax which people pay to their local authority for a dwelling is based on an estimate of the value of that dwelling. There is a banding system into which all properties, from a croft to a castle, are fitted.

- It makes no difference whether you earn nothing, £15,000 a year or £150,000 a year – you will still pay the same council tax for a Band C property in a given area.
- Poorer people may be given relief in one way or another, but that does not affect the basic nature of the tax, and is another example of subsidy for public policy purposes.

Activity 68

2 mins

List two or three other examples of indirect taxation.

_____

_____

_____

You most probably listed such items as Value Added Tax (VAT), excise duties payable on alcohol and tobacco, and the special petroleum tax added to car fuel. There are many others to choose from, including vehicle road fund licences, business rates and effectively the licence fee payable to the BBC. What they all have in common is that they take no account of ability to pay.

6.2 Every government's dilemma

Two surveys of public opinion were conducted within two weeks of each other. In the first, respondents were asked: 'Would you pay more for a better health service?'. Seventy per cent said 'yes'. In the second, the question was 'Do you want taxes to come down?'. To this, 80% responded 'yes'.

It is every government's dilemma that the electorate wants more expenditure on public services, but resents paying taxes. A majority seem to wish to have their cake and eat it and demand that governments keep on baking the cakes, even though they won't provide them with money to buy the flour, sugar, eggs and fat.

In recent times, electors seem especially to resent direct taxes which show up every week or month on their pay slips as Pay As You Earn (PAYE) deductions. This is probably why governments of all political colours have tended to shift the burden from direct to indirect taxation. After all, you don't have to buy alcohol, or petrol, or eat in restaurants, do you? So you can choose whether or not to pay the tax.

Well of course, it isn't that simple and, for many people, there is no choice but to consume at least some of the items caught by such indirect taxes as VAT. We all have to live somewhere, travel to work, buy clothes, heat our homes – all of which attract indirect taxation in one form or another.

Would governments do better to be more honest with the electorate by explaining that, while demand for health care and education can increase for ever, they can only spend ultimately what voters are prepared to let them take by way of taxation? Everyone reading this workbook is likely to be an elector, so you can judge for yourselves how you would react.

Edmund Burke, the eighteenth century reformer and philosopher said simply:

> 'In all forms of government the people is the true legislator'.

'There's nothing so certain in life as death and taxes', said the American, Benjamin Franklin. Since governments have no money, if electors 'will the ends' of welfare provisions etc., they must also 'will the means', which must be raised through taxes of one sort or another.

There seems to be no solution to the dilemma of governments as long as they face the hurdle of re-election every four or five years as in the UK. Honesty has not proved to be the best policy in the past. On the other hand, promising what you cannot deliver builds up resentment and accusations of stealth taxes when you shift from progressive direct taxes towards regressive indirect ones.

Governments can shift the tax burden towards the corporation tax (which is paid by organizations who do not have voting power in the way that individuals do). But corporations can vote with their feet by taking their businesses overseas or ceasing to invest here, thus threatening employment prospects – which will again rebound on the government.

If you remember the American company's vision of the floating factory, you'll see that the threat is real. Electorates do not like high unemployment any more than they like high taxes, and it is costly to governments.

6.3 Monetary policy

Monetary policy is the means through which governments control the economy by regulating interest rates. Money, like everything else, has its price. This is expressed as the percentage interest rate which you must pay to any lender who advances you money.

In the UK, all interest rates charged by commercial borrowers are by custom linked to the Bank of England base rate, nowadays reviewed each month. The MPC's task is to review inflationary trends against set criteria. It then sets a base rate aimed at keeping the measured rate of inflation within the tolerance limits set.

Within days of taking office in 1997, the Labour Government gave authority to the Bank of England to determine the base rate through its independent Monetary Policy Committee (MPC) which meets at the beginning of each month. The MPC was charged with using this power to keep inflation within a tightly – defined-and relatively low – inflation rate. This responsibility appears to have enabled the UK to enjoy relatively inflation-free growth for ten years.

The Government also borrows money to finance part of its expenditure, and is affected by the interest rates which it must pay to lenders. Each year, it estimates what it needs to borrow, a figure which is called the Public Sector Borrowing Requirement (PSBR).

Like any other borrower, the more the government borrows, the more interest it must pay, and the smaller the amount it has available to spend on other areas. Rising interest rates on the huge sums borrowed can have a significant effect on government finances and can hit spending on desirable projects in education, training, health, public transport, and so on.

Effects of interest rates on exchange rates

Rising interest rates will also tend to increase the value of sterling against currencies such as the dollar and the euro. This makes our exports relatively expensive and can encourage people to import foreign goods or take more overseas holidays.

Reducing interest rates has the opposite effect. This may help UK exporters but make imports and the cost of overseas travel more expensive.

6.4 How does all this affect me and the organization I work for?

The combined effects of fiscal (i.e. taxation) policies and monetary policies directly or indirectly affect every individual and every organization.

Let's begin by looking at the personal impact of the government's use of its economic levers.

Activity 69 · 5 mins

Write down two possible consequences for yourself of:

1 increasing direct taxes

_____

_____

2 increasing indirect taxes

_____

_____

3 increasing interest rates

_____

_____

4 reducing interest rates

_____

_____

What you wrote will of course reflect your own circumstances and you may wish to keep some aspects of what you have written to yourself.

Here are a few general examples of the effects which you may have covered.

1 Increasing direct taxes
Increasing direct taxes (such as PAYE and NI) reduces the amount of money available to individuals (i.e. it reduces their disposable income). This can reduce spending, demand for goods and services and possibly lead to increased unemployment. (By contrast, reducing direct taxes may have the opposite effect, but also lead to inflation – which will be discussed in Session F – if too much money is chasing too few goods and services.)

2 Increasing indirect taxes
Increasing indirect taxes (such as VAT and council tax) takes away money which people otherwise might spend on goods and services. By contrast, reducing indirect taxes may create a substantial amount of disposable income – which might fuel inflation. Such indirect taxes are regressive, they bear more heavily on people with low incomes – which may have undesirable consequences. This can cause governments to spend some of the increased tax revenues on subsidies.

3 Increasing interest rates

Increasing interest rates may cause you and millions of others to reduce what you spend on goods and services and items paid for by credit card. If you have a mortgage, the interest payable on it will take priority over holidays, new furniture and so on – especially if they too were to be financed on credit. Perhaps you might put more money into high-interest savings accounts. High interest rates may boost the value of sterling. Increased value for the pound sterling might encourage you to take holidays overseas, rather than in Great Britain.

4 Reducing interest rates

Reducing interest rates might encourage you to buy a more expensive house, or a new car – and to withdraw money from accounts paying poor rates of interest. Low interest rates may result in poor exchange rates against other currencies. A poor exchange rate against the euro may persuade you not to have a holiday abroad.

The impact of fiscal and monetary policy on your organization depends on its legal status. If you work for a public limited company, a plc, there will be published accounts which you can access, or perhaps an employees' report. Many other organizations, including charities, publish annual accounts.

6.5 Legal measures which affect economic activity

> The German unemployment figure of over 4 million (10.5% of the labour force) in August 2006 is believed to be at least in part due to the cost of labour there and the difficulty of dismissing employees, even when their jobs have become redundant. A similar situation exists in France, making many employers reluctant to invest in either country.

Virtually every law – if not **every** law, has some effect on economic activity. For example, the Health and Safety at Work etc. Act imposes conditions which affect the price of equipment and the costs of employing people, though the Act is not specifically about money.

The entire range of employment law imposes, for social and public policy reasons, conditions of employment which increase costs by comparison with developing countries which often compete with this country in the global labour market.

There are many laws devoted directly to the regulation of economic and financial activity and which do not have direct or indirect financial implications on organizations. Many of them are necessary to protect people from the activities of unscrupulous or reckless company promoters or managers. There have existed throughout history people ready and willing to part other people from their money with the promise of quick profits and low risks – an impossible combination.

While most people resent government interference in their lives and many believe that there is generally too much of it, it is essential sometimes to protect people from their own gullibility and greed and to provide punishment for those willing to exploit them.

EXTENSION 3
This extension contains a summary of some of the ways in which the government intervenes in the affairs of organizations.

Ever since 1720 there has been a succession of Companies Acts outlawing or circumscribing monopoly activities and prohibiting unfair trading practices. They are designed to force businesses to operate in a fair and honest way. It has not worked perfectly, because the villains are often cleverer than the legislators. But it is fundamentally important to the prosperity of the entire nation.

Activity 70 · 3 mins

Why do you think it is so important for business to be carried on within a strong legal framework? What can be the adverse effects if it is not?

_____

_____

_____

_____

_____

_____

The dubious accounting practices of several large US corporations, abetted by their auditors in some cases, induced just such a crisis of confidence in 2002. Many people now wonder if there is any such thing as a safe investment.

You probably answered that if there were no rules, and businesses did exactly as they pleased, then the unscrupulous would exploit every opportunity they could find to separate gullible people from their money. Though the majority of honest business people would not do so, they would become tainted with suspicion. Ultimately, confidence in business would collapse (as happened in 1721 and 1929) and business activity would threaten to grind to a halt, to no one's benefit.

It is impossible to over-estimate the importance of confidence in currencies, in governments and in the competence and honesty of business leaders.

Though businessmen grumble about all the red tape which they are tied up in, the majority of honest ones will accept that much of it is necessary and well intentioned, and scarcely impinges for most of the time on those who conduct their affairs honestly.

7 Key economic issues affecting all organizations

So far, this session has explored many of the basic elements which form the economic climate in which your organization functions. It should help you understand the issues which frequently make the headlines in the financial sections of the press. We now move on to look at some of the major economic issues that face all organizations operating in a mixed market economy.

7.1 The price mechanism

In a free market or mixed economy it is the **price mechanism** which keeps the demand and supply of the three factors of production in balance. The concept is simple:

- if supply outstrips demand, then prices will fall;
- if demand outstrips supply, then prices will rise.

The five topics introduced so far in this session are all examples of the price mechanism at work.

Activity 71

3 mins

A market trader had a large stock of bananas on his stall. He had bought them at a good price, because they were nearing the end of their saleable lives. By lunchtime, when he had sold about two thirds of them, it began to rain heavily and the customers disappeared. At three o'clock, the sun reappeared and with it the potential customers, but with only two hours maximum of trading left.

What would you have done if you were the market trader?

_____

_____

A beach ice cream vendor suffered a miserable morning of rain and chilly winds. By two o'clock most of his competitors had abandoned hope for the day and gone home. The weather relented and a glorious hot afternoon brought large numbers to the beach. The nearest cafes were more than ten minutes' hot walk away.

What might the vendor do under these circumstances?

_____

_____

No doubt you suggested that the banana seller should slash his prices and turn as much of his stock into cash as he could, selling it for whatever he could get. A rotting pile of bananas the next morning would be no use to anyone.

The beach vendor, if hard headed enough, might well exploit his local monopoly and raise prices to make back some of his lost profit from the miserable morning, and reward himself for his persistence.

These are two simple examples of market forces and the price mechanism in operation. You've almost certainly experienced similar examples – where you've obtained bargains, or gone away feeling that you've paid through the nose.

Keep these simple examples in mind as you look at the so called 'bigger issues'; at root, all markets behave similarly, if they are not distorted by factors such as subsidy or protectionism.

7.2 Exchange rates

When you travel from one country to another, the rate of exchange which you are offered reflects the purchasing power of each currency. At one time five shillings – now 25p – was often called a 'dollar', dating back to the time when the pound sterling was worth four dollars and would buy four times as much as the dollar would. Since then, the dollar has increased in value until, at the time of writing, the pound is worth around $1 50c, representing a devaluation of around 63% from that £1 = $4 rate.

When you exchange one currency for another, say pounds for euros, you are buying a commodity, just as though you were buying bananas from the market trader. What they cost reflects:

■ how badly you want to buy them;
■ how keen the seller is to sell them.

This in turn represents their purchasing power when you come to exchange them for goods and services.

This matters enormously to countries such as the UK which import and export goods and services. If the value of the pound falls against the dollar, reflecting weak economic performance here, then we have to export more goods to buy the same amount of goods priced in stronger currencies.

If the pound rises against the dollar, then we need to sell less but our exports become relatively more expensive.

If you have ever visited a country with a really weak local currency you will have experienced the anxiety of local people to acquire pounds sterling, American dollars, Swiss francs – **any** hard currency unlikely to lose its value on the currency exchanges. Over a long period of time sterling has been a relatively stable currency and this has helped the UK to remain a prosperous country. It reflects the fact that goods and services produced here are saleable and in demand from the rest of the world and also that people come here in large numbers as visitors.

Activity 72

2 mins

Imagine that you live in a country that sells one major commodity to the UK as its main source of overseas income. It buys most of the manufactured goods it needs from the UK. The total trade in each direction is around £100 million and the current exchange rate is 1 local currency unit to £1.

The local currency then falls in value by 25%, due to a failure of another crop principally exported to other countries.

By how much would the country need to increase its exports to pay for the essential items it buys from the UK?

_____

_____

_____

You will find the answer on page 209. It shows clearly the dire consequences which follow from a currency which falls in value.

If you work for an organization that imports or exports goods or services, then you will be aware how closely exchange rates are monitored. A small percentage movement in the rate can make a substantial difference to profits – or the difference between profit and loss.

7.3 Inflation

Inflation is often regarded with the same horror as cancer. Though this can be carried to extremes, there is no doubt that inflation, when it becomes rampant, can be a canker which blights the lives of millions of people.

- Germany – 1920
  In Germany, after the end of the First World War in 1918, rampant inflation (often called hyper inflation) set in, largely caused by the unrealistic demands of the Allied powers with whom she had signed the Treaty of Versailles. The Mark collapsed, losing 50% of its value in **just one day** and became eventually worthless in a country which must import many essential products. The misery and despair which this caused to millions of people was a prime factor in the rise of Hitler and National Socialism in the 1920s and 1930s and ultimately of the Second World War.

- Argentina – 2002
  For some years, the Argentine currency had been pegged to the US dollar. In reality, it was worth far less, and eventually the underlying weakness of the Argentine economy made the link untenable. The economic realities led to serious inflation, complete loss of confidence in the currency (at one time a new currency was introduced) and misery for Argentine citizens, with the threat of civil unrest constantly in the background.

These events, happening 80 years apart, illustrate the dangers of inflation which leads to the collapse of a currency. Many other examples could be quoted. Running a business becomes virtually impossible; a black market in 'hard' (i.e. trustworthy) currencies develops, and employees demand hugely increased wages to buy daily necessities whose prices are marked up daily, or sometimes hourly.

Though there have been periods of relatively steep inflation in the UK, most recently in the 1970s, this country has never experienced hyper inflation. The pound sterling has remained a relatively strong currency because of the underlying strength of the economy and a stable political system.

7.4 What causes inflation?

Nevertheless, there is continuing inflation here and many goods and services seem to move up inexorably in price, reflecting an imbalance between supply and demand.

Demand pull inflation

Demand pull inflation is what the ice cream vendor experienced on the local or 'micro' level. There were more people wishing to buy his product than he had product to sell. So, if he chose to put up his prices he could still sell his goods. On the global or 'macro' level, you can see the same effect when the supply of products like oil, which every country must have, is restricted.

Cost push inflation

The ice cream vendor's costs had not changed; he was simply increasing his price in response to increased demand.

But what if the price of ice cream, wafer biscuits, diesel fuel and road tax for his van should increase, for reasons outside his control? Then, he might eventually have to pass these costs on to his customers, simply to cover his own costs – regardless of the demand for his wares – and hope that they would still buy what is, whatever children may think, a non-essential product.

Labour-cost inflation

As you have already seen, wages, salaries, fees and so on are all ways of stating the price paid for the labour factor of production. Many trades and professions are labour intensive. The price of labour increases, the chances are that this will be passed on to consumers of goods and services and contribute to general inflation.

Trades unions that pursue successful claims are often identified with wage inflation, but non-unionized labour in occupations such as the law, sport, accountancy and politics also seek increases in payment. These can contribute to inflation, both directly and by influencing lower-paid people to seek increases on a 'me too' basis.

In the EU and other developed countries such as Australia, New Zealand, Canada and the USA, governments can contribute to labour-cost inflation by imposing 'on costs' (such as PAYE and NIC) on labour which rise steadily over the years.

It has often been said that there is no such thing as a free lunch; well there are no such things as free paid holidays, maternity leave, sick pay or time off for trade union activities.

Someone, usually the employer, has to pay, and this increases the total costs of labour. Sooner or later these costs will be passed on as higher prices, contributing to inflation.

7.5 Unemployment

Unemployment is an unpalatable fact of economic life which has been alluded to frequently in this workbook. It is a scourge for many economies and a threat to the stability of their governments. It also creates anxiety, unhappiness and loss of self esteem for many of those who find themselves out of work through no fault of their own.

In cold, economic terms, labour is a factor of production which, like any other factor, has a market price. If its cost rises above what the labour market is prepared to pay, then some of the work it does may be taken over by machines (such as computers) the cost of which can be repaid in an acceptable time by savings in labour cost.

Alternatively, in the global economy, employers may simply look for lower total labour costs overseas. A phone call takes no longer to New Delhi, Kuala Lumpur or Beijing than it does to Manchester or Belfast. Some large bookmakers have moved telephone-based activities abroad, partially for reasons connected with taxation, but also to take advantage of lower labour costs.

Much of the unemployment in the UK stems from employers seeking to replace labour with capital, or to find cheaper unit costs of labour. But unemployment can also result from:

■ the falling off, or collapse in demand for, specific activities, e.g. coal and milk delivery services are rare now that many people have central heating and buy milk from shops and supermarkets;
■ the exhaustion of raw materials or the scrapping of a process that has become too expensive or unsafe – a fact which has closed many coal mines.

Activity 73

Write down two examples each of the following causes of unemployment arising for reasons not directly concerned with the price of labour. Wherever possible, choose examples from your own experience.

Collapse in demand:

_____

_____

Exhaustion of raw materials:

_____

_____

Your answers could include a very large number of items, so it is possible only to quote a few generalized and well known examples here for you to compare them with.

Collapse in demand

Air travel has replaced ocean liners as the principal means of transporting passengers from continent to continent; central heating has replaced open fires as the chief way of heating most properties; asbestos has been replaced with other materials on health grounds; television has all but killed off many forms of live entertainment.

Exhaustion of raw materials

Many mines have run out of coal, or it has become too risky to continue mining, oil fields have run dry; much of the world's fisheries have disappeared through over fishing; some natural gas fields have already run out.

All of these matters, and any of those which you have listed, will have caused people's work to disappear. Some of them have caused enormous job losses, with profound social consequences for areas solely dependent upon them.

Of course, if suitable alternative employment is available, the effects are mitigated. But that is frequently difficult to find. If a whole area is dependent on a single occupation, such as textiles, mining, quarrying or steel-making, then it will be hard for redundant workers to find other jobs.

It would be a very brave government indeed which made full employment one of its manifesto commitments in the twenty-first century. There is no shortage of people on Earth, even if birth rates have declined in some developed countries. It becomes ever simpler to replace labour with capital as industrial robots and computer systems become ever more able to replicate human activity without becoming bored, dissatisfied or seeking higher pay or better conditions of service.

Self-assessment 5

30 mins

1   The three factors of production which every organization employs are:

_____

_____

_____

2   Suggest two reasons why organizations strive to become least cost produc-
    ers in their fields.

_____

_____

3   Which of the following represent non-renewable resources? Underline your
    selections.

solar power	natural gas	coal	timber
crude oil	iron ore	wool	sea fish

4   Other things being equal, the more _____ a factor of production
    becomes, the _____ will be its _____ price.

5   If the cost of labour becomes relatively _____, organizations will
    seek to _____ it with _____ equipment, or by finding
    people prepared to _____.

6   Explain in your own words what you understand by the word 'monopoly'.

7   What adverse effects can the use of subsidies have on the work of the price
    mechanism? Allowing for this, do you believe that there are circumstances
    where state subsidies can be justified?

_____

_____

_____

_____

8 Give two examples of indirect competition which could affect the activities of:

■ a bus operator in London, Manchester or Newcastle

_____

_____

■ a fish-and-chip shop

_____

_____

■ a cinema

_____

_____

9 The levying of _____ taxes, such as income tax and _____ tax, are examples of the government's _____ policies in action.

10 Indirect taxes, such as _____ and _____ are deemed to be _____ because they bear more heavily on people with _____ incomes.

11 Every government's dilemma concerning fiscal policy is that the electorate demand higher and higher levels of ___ _____ _____, but are unwilling to see _____ rise to pay for them.

12 Exchange rates measure the relative _____ power of two _____ and indicate the _____ strength of their economies.

13 Give one example each of:

■ cost push inflation;   _____
■ demand pull inflation; _____
■ wage-related inflation. _____

14 Unemployment can arise from causes such as the _____ of natural resources, the _____ of labour with _____ equipment, or the _____ of activities elsewhere in pursuit of _____ labour.

15 Uncontrolled or _____ inflation inevitably leads to _____ unemployment, which can _____ governments and lead to _____ gaining power.

Answers to these questions can be found on pages 203–4.

8 Summary

- The economic and political decisions of governments affect every business and every individual in the community so everyone should take a close interest in them.

- Factors beyond governments' control, such as natural disasters and the decisions of multinational corporations, can have a profound effect on the economy in the short and longer term.

- The UK has a mixed economy in which central government retains responsibility for essential services such as health, but most goods and services are provided by privately run profit-seeking organizations.

- It is the price mechanism which keeps demand and supply in balance in a mixed economy.

- The global economy now allows and encourages businesses to move from one country, or continent, to another if the price of land, capital and labour exceeds levels which they are willing to pay. Manufacturing and administrative jobs are both affected by this trend.

- Subsidies, whether for political, social policy, or other reasons, distort the price mechanism and can cause problems to both providers and receivers in the longer term.

- Monopolistic practices, which also distort the price mechanism, are either banned or tightly controlled in the UK to prevent exploitation and profiteering.

- The government uses taxes (fiscal policy) and control of interest rates (monetary policy) to control inflationary trends.

- The government has no money of its own; it can spend only what the electorate is willing for it to raise through taxes.

- The dilemma of successive governments has been that electors desire better public services but resent paying taxes which provide the means of paying for them.

- In many countries rampant inflation has led to the collapse of currencies, unemployment on a vast scale, civil unrest and the election of extremist governments.

- Many laws stipulating what organizations can and cannot do have been enacted over centuries to protect the general public against the activities of unscrupulous businessmen.

- A stable economy, in which inflation is contained, the currency keeps its value and unemployment is the exception, provides the right climate for social stability and a democratic society. Only in such conditions can a government provide services such as health, state pensions, education and welfare, which have come to be accepted as the norm in the UK.

Session F
The global village

1 Introduction

Session E introduced the basic concepts and principles which define and underlie economic activities, almost regardless of how politicians and organizations try to influence them. You will find it very helpful to keep the basics in mind during this session, where the outlook widens to the world issues which influence all organizations here in the short, medium and long term.

The UK has long been a trading nation. Evidence of this is to be seen in countless ways. Here are just a few examples.

■ Saffron cake is very popular in Cornwall. Saffron, a prized ingredient of Indian and Central Asian food, is thought to have been introduced to Cornwall by Phoenician traders perhaps hundreds of years B.C., who took tin from local mines back to their eastern Mediterranean lands.

■ Dundee has been associated with marmalade for centuries. The Seville oranges from which it is made are almost exclusively imported to the UK. In World War Two special arrangements were made to secure supplies, as marmalade was believed important to maintaining morale.

■ Before the Panama Canal was opened in 1914 linking the Atlantic and Pacific Oceans, sailing ships carried coal from ports in South Wales around the perilous Cape Horn, returning laden with guano from Chile. The guano, a fertilizer provided free by millions of sea birds, was used to fertilize arable farms here. The round trip under sail involved over 20,000 miles of peril and hardship.

■ Flax grown in Northern Ireland's mild, moist climate was made into linen, then transformed into high quality fabrics and clothing for export throughout the world.

- In Norfolk and Suffolk the beautiful 'wool' churches are evidence of the medieval wool trade with continental Europe. Many of the weavers here were Huguenot refugees who had escaped from persecution in Europe.
- Joseph Banks, a scientist who sailed with the explorer Captain Cook in the eighteenth century, helped to found Kew Gardens, which was instrumental in transplanting rubber and tea to Malaysia and India respectively.
- Scottish malts are prized by connoisseurs of whisky. They have been an important source of foreign exchange for centuries, and remain so to this day.

2 The UK's international trade

2.1 Visible and invisible trade

The above examples illustrate the scope and variety of international trade to and from the UK. They can be divided into two categories for statistical purposes:

- 'visible';
- 'invisible'.

Visible items are products which have **tangible** (or physical) form. Examples we have discussed so far include imports of saffron, Seville oranges and guano, and exports of whisky, wool, coal, tin and clothing.

Invisible items are **intangible** (non-physical) and often take the form of a service or financial product. The invisible imports in the above illustrations included payments for services (the expertise of drainage engineers and weavers) and, for exports, expertise in railway construction and horticulture, which also brought longer-term benefits.

Activity 74

3 mins

List some other examples of visible and invisible trade, with as many as possible drawn from your own experience and that of your organization. Classify your examples into imports and exports and, wherever possible, give specific items rather than broad categories.

Imports		Exports	
Invisibles	**Visibles**	**Invisibles**	**Visibles**

> In this workbook one billion is taken to mean one thousand million, as this is used in all official figures such as the *Annual Abstract of Statistics*.

On page 209 you will find a completed grid, simply for comparison with your own.

You may have found that it was harder to think of individual examples of invisible items than of visible goods which the UK imports and exports.

Your lists could have included a huge variety of items. Selecting them should have helped get you into the right frame of mind for exploring the fascinating and complex issues of international trade and the global issues challenging the UK.

2.2 The balance of visible trade

Overall, in the year 2001, The UK:

- **exported** £191,000,000,000 of tangible goods – known as £191 billion by the American way of calculating one billion
- **imported** £224,000,000,000 of tangible goods – or £224 billion.

EXTENSION 4
A useful source of statistics is the Government's Annual Abstract Of Statistics, available from The Stationery Office.

That left a **balance of trade** deficit of £33 billion – a vast sum to be in the red.

The figures are so enormous, and the process for collecting the data so prone to error, that it would be foolhardy to believe that they are precise. As you saw in Session E, the much quoted figure for inflation has to be viewed carefully, as in reality every individual and organization has a unique inflation rate.

Benjamin Disraeli, a nineteenth-century British Prime Minister, said:

'there are lies, damned lies and statistics'.

However, because the trade figures are so large, the chances are that there will be as many errors in one direction as another and many will probably cancel each other out, rather like the decisions of umpires and referees in sport. Players never seem to remember the times when they were fortunate. Over time good and bad decisions tend to cancel themselves out, if they are honestly made.

The trouble with official statistics is that politicians try to interpret them to prove that they are right and their opponents wrong. This can influence the way in which figures are collected and presented. But the sheer volume of figures is against their discrediting the figures entirely.

2.3　The balance on invisible items

Because of the size of the UK's balance of trade deficit in regard to visible earnings, its nett earnings from invisible items are extremely important. For many years, they more than compensated for the adverse trade gap between imports and exports of visible items.

In 2001, the UK had a surplus on the invisible items of £13,000,000,000, or £13 billion. This continues the pattern of many years, and reflects the UK's expertise in financial services and its popularity with tourists.

2.4　The balance of payments

The balance of payments brings together the figures for visible and invisible items to strike an overall balance each year – in simple terms not unlike a company profit and loss account. Bringing in the surplus on invisible items reduces the deficit on visible trade to an overall payments deficit of £20,000,000,000 – £20 billion – still a huge number.

EXTENSION 5
This extension summarizes some of the main figures from international trade, from which you will see how enormous the sums are. The statistical law of 'inertia of large numbers' states that large groups of data are more stable and reliable than small ones, so the figures should give a reasonably true picture.

2.5 Trends in balance of trade and balance of payments

In Extension 5 (pages 195–6) you will find the figures for the years 1997 to 2001 accumulated. They show that:

- the total deficit on visible trade for five years was £123 billion;
- the total balance of payments deficit for the same period was £63 billion.

2.6 The possible effects on the sterling exchange rate

Over a period of time the tendency for deficits to increase is worrying because it could put pressure on the value of the pound sterling. For the present, the deficit is being financed and virtually eliminated by other items, such as flows of investment capital. The relatively high interest rates maintained for several years by the Bank of England MPC have tended to maintain the exchange rate.

However, in the longer term it is essential for the UK to balance its books if it is to retain its prosperity and political influence in the world, just as any organization – public, private, or charitable – must.

The statistical data has been presented at the very start of this session because it shows clearly how vital international trade is to the UK economy. Since the whole of the session is concerned with European and international issues, it is as well to have a picture of the colossal figures involved in the UK's trade from the outset.

More detail will be added as the session progresses, providing you with breakdowns of the total figures to show clearly:

- what we export and to whom;
- what we import and from where.

It is surprising how many organizations are involved in exporting and importing, in ways you may not expect. For example:

■ if an NHS hospital treats overseas patients who pay for the services directly, or through a health insurance scheme, that will count as an export;
■ the same hospital may source drugs from foreign countries, which are imports;
■ a call centre may buy equipment from overseas, which is an import, but sell insurance services by phone to foreign buyers, which then count as exports;
■ a department store may import large quantities of goods from around the world and resell some of them, together with UK-produced items to foreign tourists, which represent exports.

The effect of exchange rates on organizations

Imagine a paper company imports £5 millions' worth of wood pulp and exports £1.5 millions' worth of paper products, selling the remainder of its output in the UK. So the organization has a personal balance of trade deficit of £3.5 million.

Now, visualize a fall in the value of sterling of 5%, so that each £1 is worth only 95 pence.

The cost of imported pulp will now be (100/95 × 5,000,000) or £5,263,158 – over a quarter of a million pounds more, because each £1 buys 5% less.

The value of the exports will now be (95/100 × 1,500,000) or £1,425,000 – a fall of £75,000 in value because the overseas importer needs to spend only 95% of the former cost to buy the same amount of pounds to pay for the goods.

Five per cent is a very significant loss of value for a currency, especially if it happens rapidly. But it is trivial compared with the falls which have happened in countries such as Germany and Argentina, described in Session E, or in Italy, France, Brazil and Turkey. You may have visited countries where it has happened and seen at first hand the anxiety and near panic which it can cause.

In the example, the company is both importing and exporting. It is adding value to its exports and selling finished products for three times the cost of the imported raw materials – £300 per tonne as compared with £100 per tonne.

Many organizations of course do just that; most things in economics are not straightforward.

An organization which imports raw materials, processes them and sells on the finished goods will have to run faster to stay where it is by either selling more as the currency value depreciates, or by increasing prices, if the market will bear it. But, as you have seen in Session E, competition and the price mechanism may not allow it to do so.

If you are solely an importer, say of American wines, then you may find that your entire business is badly hit by a fall in the value of sterling, which you are powerless to influence. Conversely, if you are an exporter, you may find that an increase in value of sterling will hit your sales, as your customers find it more expensive to buy pounds to pay you with.

Unless your own organization uses no imported goods or services (which is unlikely given that the UK imports now exceed £200 billion per year) and is without export earnings (more likely, but exports averaged £175 billion over the years 1997 to 2001), then movements in exchange rates will have a very significant effect – for good or ill.

The UK has avoided catastrophic falls in the value of sterling, but the upward trend in balance of payments deficits must raise long-term concerns about it and the prosperity which goes with a stable currency in which people throughout the world have confidence.

The answer is, as always, for an island nation not self sufficient in resources, and dependent on the skills and ingenuity of its people:

- to export relatively more;
- to import relatively less;
- to remain outward looking and aware that, in the medium to long term, you can't spend what you don't earn.

> In 2000, 21% of UK household income came from payments made by the State. This is an increase of more than 10% over 15 years under succeeding Conservative and Labour Governments. Such spending, however desirable it may be, can only be afforded by a financially sound economy.

3 The UK's trading partners

The simplest and quickest way to see with whom the UK trades is to open a world atlas. Look at the overall projection of the world and the six continents inhabited by several billion potential customers and suppliers. There is hardly a place on earth that has no trade links with this country.

3.1 The United Nations (UN)

At the beginning of 2003, the UN had 191 member states and it would be hard to find any that the UK does not trade with, short of embargoes or insurmountable tariff barriers being imposed.

3.2 The British Commonwealth

There are more than 50 Commonwealth countries with whom the UK has close political, trading and cultural links. They include wealthy, developed nations such as Australia and Canada on the one hand and some of the world's poorest countries, for example, Sierra Leone, on the other. Trade with the UK is vital to the poorer countries, which may depend on exports of commodities such as bananas, cocoa, coffee, copper or iron ore, and cane sugar.

3.3 The United States of America (USA)

The USA has a land area of more than 9 million square kilometres and a population in 2002 estimated at 276 million – just over 30 people per square kilometre. By comparison, the area of Europe, including European Russia, is 10 million square kilometres and its population is estimated at more than 700 million – 70 people per square kilometre. The area of the UK is 244 square kilometres and its population is nearly 60 million – 245 people per square kilometre.

The USA has the world's largest single economy and is the dominant power in world economics and politics. Many multinational companies are based there and many of the technologies that affect farming, pharmaceuticals and other activities throughout the world have been developed there.

With the demise of the USSR as a true world power, following the near collapse of its centrally directed economy and division into many individual states, the USA is the only true super power left at present.

The USA has enormous economic advantages. The next activity invites you to suggest what they may be.

Activity 75 · 3 mins

List up to five economic factors which you believe the USA has in its favour compared with European countries. Think in terms of factors of production – land, labour, capital and natural resources to guide your selections.

_____

_____

_____

_____

_____

You will find some suggestions against which to compare your own in Extension 6. They are so numerous that it is not surprising that the US is so dominant in world affairs.

EXTENSION 6
This extension comprises a brief survey of the USA's intrinsic economic advantages.

The USA rouses strong emotions concerning its economic, foreign and defence policies. The activities of multinationals, ranging from Walt Disney to Exxon, from McDonalds to Monsanto, Microsoft and the communications giant AOL Time Warner, penetrate everywhere on earth.

Whatever views other countries may hold about the USA, it would be a grave mistake to ignore it. Every country in the world will continue to be affected by the policies framed in Washington and the industrial and commercial power houses of California, Detroit, Chicago, New York and Seattle.

The information given here about the European Union is based on the actual membership of 25 states in 2006. Five other countries have 'candidate' status: Romania, Bulgaria, Croatia, FYR Macedonia and Turkey at this time.

The USA continues to be the UK's largest single trading partner, despite the 3,000 miles of Atlantic Ocean which divide the two countries (compared with 22 miles of English Channel between England and France). This shows how strong the necessity is to trade with such a giant economic power, which was also our ally in two world wars. Analysis of the remaining EU countries would show that they too have strong trading links across the Atlantic, however great the political gulf may be.

3.4 The European Union (EU)

EXTENSION 7
Extension 7 gives a full list of actual EU member states and an indication of some potential new members.

In fact, the Treaty of Nice states that **any** European State which has a democratic system of government may join, so there can be no definitive list.

The EU already comprises 27 European states, some of them very large economies in their own right, including our own and those of Germany, France and Italy.

In Extension 7, you will find a complete list of current members. The EU, one of the most powerful groups of trading nations on earth, will be examined in detail in section 4 of this session.

3.5 Other major nations and continents with whom we trade

Other partners with whom the UK trades include:

- Russia and the former USSR satellite republics in Asia, with economies currently in various states of development following the rapid demise of centralized communist power in the 1980s and 1990s;
- the oil exporting countries of the Middle East, crucial to the world economy and currently highly dependent on a single commodity for their prosperity;
- China, the most populous country on earth, which now includes Hong Kong and which is keen to expand trade with western nations;
- South America, with the huge countries of Mexico, Brazil, Chile and Argentina; having vast resources on the one hand and grinding poverty on the other;
- Japan and the so-called Pacific rim countries such as South Korea and Taiwan which are emerging as major manufacturing countries.

The former USSR has split into many states, including many which are economically underdeveloped and often beset by border disputes and even civil war. The former USSR republics include: Azerbaijan; Belarus; Dagestan; Georgia; Chechnya; Armenia; Ukraine; Uzbekistan; Turkmenistan; Kyrgystan and Kazakhstan.

The UK's worst imbalance of trade is with Japan, a country which relies on ingenuity and manufacturing expertise and has few natural resources of its own. Together with China and the Pacific rim countries, Japan accounts for £17.6 billion – well over half – of our enormous £30 billion deficit on visible trade in 2000 – a proportion which is almost certainly increasing.

In Extension 5, you will find a table summarizing all of the UK's visible trade with the whole world. The figures are broken down:

- firstly by the broad categories of goods which we import and export;
- secondly to show our largest trading partners and the individual balance of trade surpluses or deficits which we have with them.

Few Commonwealth countries are specifically listed in the table. Most appear in the Other countries category, with whom collectively the UK has a £10 billion trade deficit.

It is important to remember that, although in UK trade terms imports and exports from countries like Nigeria, Zambia, Guyana, Sri Lanka and other Commonwealth countries may be relatively small, our imports from them may be a major source of local employment and foreign exchange – or simply survival.

Other European countries – France, Spain, Portugal and Belgium in particular – have strong historical and commercial links to former colonies throughout the world and a long history of reciprocal trading with them, often vital to local economies.

To complete the next activity, you will need to study the figures provided in Extension 5. They may contain some surprises.

> The UK's balance of visible trade deficit is larger than many developing countries' total outputs of goods and services.

Activity 76 · 10 mins

Study Table (c) in Extension 5, then write down:

> The economy of California alone is reckoned to be among the largest in the world, even though at the start of 2003 it was technically bankrupt! It is as big as the economies of some countries. California has an area of more than 400,000 square kilometres and a population of nearly 34 million.

1   with which country we had the largest trade **deficit** and how large it was

_____

2   with which country we had the largest trade **surplus** and how great the surplus was

_____

3   taking the far eastern countries of China, Hong Kong, South Korea and Taiwan, the total deficit that the UK has with them

_____

4   the total you arrived at in question 3 as a percentage of the total UK deficit of £30 billion

_____

5   with which countries the UK's trade is in balance, i.e. having a surplus or deficit of less than £1 billion

_____

6   the largest **single** trading partner which the UK has and the total of the import and export trade with it

_____

The answers can be found on pages 209–10.

3.6 The world's sole economic super power

The answer to the last question in Activity 75 once again shows how important the UK's trading relationship with the USA is, a fact which would be true for a high percentage of all the UN's 191 member states.

The next section looks more closely at the EU and its institutions, which are of vital importance to the UK and its well being. However, this section has shown clearly that global issues are equally important in the long term and that the economic dominance of the USA cannot be ignored.

Just before we turn to European matters, the following true case study illustrates just how ramified trading patterns now are.

> The IKEA furniture company is based in Almhult, a small town, 300 miles from Stockholm in Sweden. From small beginnings it has grown into a business with 170 stores and 70,000 employees in many countries. Its annual turnover now approaches 10 billion euros, or £6.5 billion. Some other statistics are as follows:
>
> - its headquarters are in Sweden, which is a member of the EU;
> - the store with the largest individual turnover is in London, exceeding £130 million annually;
> - Germany produces the highest sales in total for an individual country;
> - it uses approximately 2,000 suppliers in 55 countries, including 15 EU members;
> - the principal suppliers are in Sweden itself – and China whose trade with western nations is, as you have seen from the UK figures, of growing significance.

Activity 77 · 3 mins

Look at the IKEA case study and say how you expect that the company's activities might affect:

- the UK's balance of visible trade with Sweden;
- Germany's balance of visible trade with Sweden;
- UK exports of visible trade items;
- Sweden's balance of visible trade with China;
- the exchange rate of sterling against the Swedish Krona.

_____

_____

_____

_____

_____

You will find the answers on page 210.

As with most questions on trade and economics, there are no definitive answers of the $2 + 2 = 4$ variety. Other factors also come into it, such as the possible creation of retail and manufacturing jobs in the UK, which you were not asked to consider.

The IKEA company will probably be known to many readers, either as customers or perhaps through working for one of their 2,000 suppliers. Though the company is very large by normal standards, the effect which it will have **individually** on international trade and exchange rates is limited.

However, when you add up the activities of such companies – and the much larger ones in petrochemicals, vehicle manufacturing, pharmaceuticals, agriculture – then the decisions of private organizations begin to have a really significant effect on whole economies, and may be taken independently of any political or social concerns of national governments.

4 The European Union (EU)

4.1 A brief history 1952 – 2006

The European Coal & Steel Community (ECSC) was formed in 1952 and consisted of France, Germany, Holland, Italy, Luxembourg and Belgium – countries which had all suffered dreadfully from the wars which ravaged Europe over the centuries.

The original impetus for the formation of a European trading bloc was the desire to rescue Europe from a seemingly endless round of wars and prohibitive expenditure on defence.

France and Germany had been at war in 1870, 1914 and again in 1939. Even between the two World Wars, there had been an invasion of part of Germany by France, and a history of mistrust and hatred prevailed which seemed to have no end.

Italy, like Germany, had been governed by a brutal dictatorship between the World Wars. It had been allied to Hitler's Germany and eventually suffered a crushing defeat and the ruination of much of its industrial base and historic heritage.

Ypres, a beautiful city in Belgium, is associated forever with the unimaginable horrors of trench warfare and mindless waste of life in World War One rather than the splendour of its medieval cloth hall and its dedication to trade.

During World War Two millions of people died throughout Europe, and appalling destruction was wrought on historic cities, towns and buildings from Berlin to Antwerp and from St. Malo to Rotterdam.

In 1955, the 'group of six', as the original member states of the EU became known, agreed to establish a wider common market in goods, services and people. Two years later the Treaty of Rome gave legal effect to the European Economic Community, or EEC, which came into being in 1958.

Since then, the Community has widened until it now includes the 27 member states listed in Extension 7. The UK joined following a referendum in 1973. The UK was initially reluctant to become involved in what was perceived by most leaders here as the beginning of some kind of potential European super state.

There were concerns here about the potential effects on Commonwealth nations with whom the UK had long histories of mutual assistance – including during time of war – and on the special relationship with the USA which had twice intervened to assist this country during the two World Wars.

The UK had not been invaded or defeated in either war. It had suffered considerable loss of life, and destruction of much of its historic heritage in many towns and cities through aerial bombardments by the German Luftwaffe's aircraft and V1 and V2 rockets.

Furthermore, the British constitution, systems of government and law were very different to their European counterparts and had evolved separately over nearly a thousand years.

4.2 UK trade with EU countries

Collectively, the UK does over half its total trade with the other EU member states.

The problem with all statistics that have political implications is that politicians try to present them in a way that supports their own objectives. So, for example:

- a pro-Europe British politician will wish to stress the value of UK trade with the EU, whereas
- a Eurosceptic will wish to emphasize the UK's trade beyond Europe.

What both of them should accept is that trade with the European mainland is vital to the UK's continuing prosperity. A stable, peaceful Europe is vital to the UK's national interests.

4.3 The Eurozone

The American economy illustrates the value of a single currency. In the USA the dollar is in use among 300 million people across a federation of 50 states. In addition, it is used as both a trading and a reserve currency throughout the world.

The Roman Empire, which lasted for centuries, also used a single currency – from North Africa to Northern Europe.

In January 2002 most European currencies were replaced with a single currency. The euro is now used by more than 300 million people, and by 2006 it had started to establish itself as an international benchmark currency to rival the dollar.

Only Sweden, Denmark and the UK are still outside this 'Eurozone'. The Danish electorate voted against joining in a referendum held in 2000; the UK government has yet to hold such a referendum. The UK government announced a series of economic tests which must be passed before the choice of whether or not to join is put to a referendum in England, Northern Ireland, Scotland and Wales at an unspecified date.

Once again, it is impossible to distinguish between the political, cultural and economic considerations which have influenced the views of those countries which adopted the euro and those, Sweden, Denmark and the UK, which did not. There is probably greater suspicion of the motives underlying moves towards monetary union in these countries than in the other states of Europe. There is also perhaps more long-term confidence in sterling than there was in the franc or the lira, both of which at some time suffered catastrophic falls in value during the twentieth century. Sterling has never collapsed, although it has depreciated significantly against the dollar over a period of many years (which has included two costly wars).

4.4 The EU's key institutions

The Council of Ministers

The Council of Ministers is the key decision-making body in the EU and comprises one minister drawn from each of the member countries, regardless of its size or economic stature. The UK government's key representative is normally the Foreign Secretary, although other ministers will attend certain meetings instead, according to the topic being discussed. The Council is normally chaired by each EU country in turn, for a six-month period.

The Council is not in permanent session, as a national government would be, but meets on an ad hoc basis. Although the ministers are nominated to the Council by their own governments rather than being elected to it directly, they have been elected in their own countries as members of their own parliaments.

The European Commission

In effect, the Commission is equivalent to the Civil Service in the UK. It consists of a number of Commissioners appointed by member states for a four-year term which is renewable. Commissioners are not elected and most of them are former politicians. The Commission has a president, who normally holds the office for four years before being replaced by someone of a different nationality.

The Commissioners are pledged to take a Europe-wide view of issues and not to represent simply their own country's interests.

The Commission has several functions:

- to make proposals on recommended courses of action to the Council of Ministers
- to implement the decisions of the Council
- to promote the EU's interests in defined ways.

The Commissioners are supported in Brussels by a large bureaucracy, which does research into areas of potential interest to the EU and assists with implementing and monitoring decisions taken.

The European Parliament

This is the only EU body whose members are elected **directly** by their own constituents in their own countries, though the constituency boundaries are much wider than those of the national ones. They are now elected by proportional representation.

The UK has 87 Members of the European Parliament (MEPs), as compared with 659 MPs elected to Westminster.

The Parliament can dismiss the Commissioners and has some powers over the way in which the vast EU budget is spent.

The European Court of Justice

This European Court of Justice is responsible for applying European Treaties and interpreting and adjudicating on disputes which may arise. The judges' decisions are binding on each member state, taking precedence over decisions made in its own courts. As such, they are a continuing source of friction between the Court in Luxembourg and EU Governments.

(Note that the European Court of Justice is a totally different court from the European Court of Human Rights – which is not an EU institution.)

The EU Budget and the Common Agricultural Policy (CAP)

The Commission's budgetary figures for 2006 show that the EU budget will total (108.4 bn (72.6 bn), equivalent to one third of the UK's total visible exports. This money is contributed by the 25 member states and spent for agreed purposes through the Commission's administration.

Some 40% of the budget is spent on the Common Agricultural Policy (CAP), which is a lower proportion than in some previous years.

At one time more than 50% of the EU's budget went on the CAP. The policy is of course much easier to attack in 2006, when most Europeans have no real idea what it is like to be hungry.

Fifty years earlier, the CAP was born out of food shortages in post-war Europe and memories of near-starvation in World War Two. The intention was to achieve self sufficiency in food production for the original six member states, an objective which was achieved.

However, other aspects of the policy, such as the imposition of tariffs on non-EU countries and the creation of vast surpluses in the 1980s, have made it the most contentious aspect of EU policy, and successive Commissions and Councils of Ministers have said that they will reform it.

4.5 Does any of this matter to the UK?

You are recommended to look at broadsheet newspapers such as *The Times, The Guardian, The Daily Telegraph, The Independent, The Scotsman, The Herald (Glasgow), The Press and Journal (Aberdeen), The Western Mail* and *The Financial Times* or their Sunday equivalents, on a regular basis – and to listen to BBC Radio 4 or World Service broadcasts which provide regular, authoritative and approachable accounts of the EU and world affairs.

The way in which the EU's budget is funded and spent certainly matter to the UK.

The aspects of life in the UK which decisions taken by European institutions can affect include:

■ hours of work and general working conditions;
■ price of food and how it is to be produced;
■ food hygiene;
■ employment law;
■ standards applied to health and safety;
■ environmental law;
■ quotas for fisheries;
■ weights and measures;
■ immigration and emigration to and from the UK;
■ the overall shape of farming and the nature of the countryside.

All these matters can affect employment, the cost of living and the quality of life here. The UK has around a sixth of the total present EU population – 60 million out of 380 millions. That, plus its economic strengths and influence in the world, demand that its collective voice should be heard, based on rational opinions formed by as many as possible of the electorate here.

5 International organizations which influence the UK

5.1 The World Bank

The World Bank comprises the International Bank for Reconstruction and Development (IBRD) and the International Development Association (IDA). Its function is primarily to assist developing countries. Loans are made on a reasonably commercial basis. The Bank will assess each project proposed – perhaps a hydro electric scheme or the development of a new port – and assure itself that the investment will yield a return sufficient to pay interest and, over time, the capital advanced as well. The profits are used to fund developmental projects.

Desirable schemes which are not designed to yield commercial returns can be financed by the IDA, the other part of the World Bank.

The IDA takes a less commercial view than the IBRD. For example, it may provide money for educational and agricultural projects for which the short-term benefits are less certain, but which may produce great long-term ones to countries too poor to fund them.

5.2 The International Monetary Fund (IMF)

Like the World Bank, the IMF was founded in 1945. Its purpose was to encourage the expansion of world trade and make loans to countries to help them overcome balance of payments difficulties which, if uncorrected, would threaten their currency. The aim was to avoid the catastrophic collapses in the value of currencies which are frequently linked to political turmoil, the onset of dictatorial rule and potentially to the outbreak of war.

While this has helped many states, including the UK, to overcome difficulties, the conditions which the IMF attaches to loans and its power to affect a country's internal affairs often cause controversy.

Brazil, Argentina's northern neighbour, the largest country in South America and one of the world's ten largest economies, has experienced similar problems leading to a fall of more than 20% in the exchange rate of the Brazilian currency, the real, against the dollar.

In August 2001 the IMF lent $8 billion to the Argentine government to help it make loan repayments which would otherwise have been beyond its capacity. The IMF attached conditions to the loan which it deemed some months later had not been met. It therefore refused to pay the December instalment. The country was plunged into crisis, with foreign debts totalling $141 billion and adult unemployment standing at 18%. The peso was devalued a few weeks later by 30%. The President declared Argentina bankrupt – in other words, unable to meet its international debts. Emergency financial measures imposed by the government led to rioting and the threat of political instability.

5.3 What has this to do with the UK and its business organizations?

You may well ask what this has to do with the organization for which you work. After all, these events were occurring thousands of miles away.

That's true, but it has happened here too. In 1967 the UK was forced to devalue the pound from a fixed value of $2.80 to $2.40 (around 8.5%) as a condition imposed by the IMF for continuing assistance to the UK economy. The pound was over-valued and did not truly reflect what it would purchase from countries which were using strong currencies such as the Swiss franc, the Japanese yen or the dollar.

The Prime Minister at the time, Harold Wilson, announced on television that 'the pound in your pocket is worth the same as before'.

Was he right in 1967 and, if so, does the same apply to the Argentinian peso or the Brazilian real? The following activity will help you decide.

Activity 78 · 8 mins

Imagine three different Argentinian businesses:

■ a company which exports 5 million pesos' worth of wine to the UK;
■ a company which imports North Sea Oil worth 20 million pesos;
■ a market trader who buys produce locally and sells it via market stalls in Rio de Janeiro. He buys 75,000 pesos' worth each period and re-sells for 150,000 pesos.

What effect would a devaluation of the peso of 30% have on each business?

_____

_____

_____

The answer can be found on page 210.

Because the market trader buys and sells locally and deals only in the local currency, the devaluation has no direct effect on this business. But what happens if he has to buy imported diesel fuel for his vehicles, or a new van imported from Japan or Germany?

The peso in his pocket will then buy a lot less than it did before, even if his overseas supplier is willing to accept a currency in which confidence has been lost.

5.4 The World Trade Organization (WTO)

The aim of the WTO is to promote trade among all the world's nations, free of artificial tariff barriers erected to protect local businesses in some countries. Based in Geneva, its remit covers services, physical goods and intellectual property.

In 1995, the World Trade Organization (WTO) succeeded the General Agreement on Tariffs and Trade (GATT), which had similar aims and objectives.

Its role is a sensitive one, for it is often required to arbitrate between the competing interests of individual countries or the richer nations as a group and the poorer ones which depend on them as export markets for commodities such as rubber, coffee (of which the USA, for example, is a nett importer), bananas, rice, cocoa and metal ores.

The WTO faces dilemmas in:

- agriculture;
- textiles;
- clothing.

It could have a significant effect on your organization's business if it is involved in any way, directly or indirectly, in these business sectors.

5.5 The Organisation for Economic Co-operation and Development (OECD)

The OECD comprises 30 member countries which between them produce two-thirds of the world's goods and services (they are also, of course, involved with the WTO and the UN). As the name suggests, the OECD is involved with channelling support to developing nations, many of whom have strong cultural and economic ties already to European states such as Spain, Portugal and France. It is much concerned with issues affecting international commerce, including biotechnology, sustainable development and food safety.

5.6 Globalization and the multinational corporations

All the bodies so far described are run by, or on behalf of, countries. They are well known and many of their activities are fairly public. They are not profit making, in the sense that they have no shareholders to whom they owe a duty to optimize profits.

But in recent years many huge multinational corporations, largely privately owned, have developed which are very powerful and influential in world politics and economics.

When did Globalization begin?

Multinationals are not a new phenomenon. The eighteenth-century East India Company was one of the mainsprings of the British Empire.

In later centuries, British and French engineers helped to build railways, canals, roads and other infrastructure projects throughout the world. When oil became the dominant source of energy, the companies which tapped this vast resource had to be internationally minded. Many of the countries which used oil had none of their own and had to operate overseas.

Shipping companies have always been global in character. This has led to benefits to marine safety standards that are generally recognized throughout the world, saving countless lives at sea. Similar safety benefits flowed from the globalization of air traffic control, at the instigation of public and private airlines.

Why is it so contentious now?

How has so much changed to make the operations of modern multinationals a subject of so much debate and acrimony?

The UK itself has received large-scale overseas investment from many countries. You may work for an organization from overseas yourself and so have personal experience to draw upon.

People don't forget that disasters such as the Exxon Valdez oil spillage in Alaska, the Bhopal chemical plant explosion in India and Thalidomide in the UK and other countries, all resulted from the failures of international corporations.

Is it all about cheap labour?

No labour is cheap if it cannot do the job to the right quality standards, so it isn't that simple, but standards are improving all the time. Car plants in South Korea and Taiwan work to the same stringent standards as European ones and are just as likely to have the equivalent of ISO 9000 quality systems.

As far as protecting the environment is concerned, an increasing number of Asian manufacturers work to the environmental standard equivalent of ISO 14001, so it may be unfair to accuse all Pacific rim companies of ravaging their environments and adding to the Asian cloud of pollution which featured in much media coverage in 2002.

Universal English – a two edged sword?

English has become virtually the universal language of commerce, a great boon and blessing to English and American business people who are unable or unwilling to learn other languages. But is there a downside for us in having a large percentage of the world's population speaking English?

The ease of communication which makes it simple for English speakers to communicate throughout the world can rebound on such countries as the USA and the UK since other countries, now including China, see the teaching of English as encouraging inward investment, and therefore benefiting their economies at the expense of the traditionally English-speaking nations.

5.7 International crime

While the multinational corporations provide legitimate employment, pay taxes and can be held legally accountable in the countries in which they operate, there is one increasingly influential aspect of international trade which cannot be ignored.

As the people who engage in international crime render no accounts, pay no taxes and recognize no laws, no statistics are available to show how much the trade amounts to. Nevertheless, every estimate made shows that hundreds or thousands of billions of pounds are involved each year.

Activity 79 · 3 mins

Suggest what some of the main areas of international crime might be, and how they might affect the UK's economic activity. Indicate if your own organization suffers ill effects specifically from any of them.

_____

_____

_____

_____

International crime is involved in most or all of the activities which legitimate businesses deal with, so the list could be a long one. Some of the most lucrative and most threatening for organizations and governments are:

- illegal drugs – now one of the world's largest international trades;
- counterfeit goods – CDs, designer brands, computer software;
- armaments – a vast trade, fuelled by the break-up of the former Soviet Union;
- smuggling of items carrying high excise duties – tobacco, alcohol, fuel;
- people – for purposes including illegal immigration, slave labour, vice;

- piracy – which is increasing in frequency in various parts of the world;
- kidnapping for ransom – endemic in some countries and a great deterrent to investment by legitimate businesses.

The effect on legitimate organizations and markets throughout the world can be enormous. For example:

- illegal drugs can reduce or destroy the effectiveness of employees, cause crime and increase taxes spent on preventive measures;
- trade in counterfeit CDs, videos, smuggled goods and people can have serious financial effects on organizations, reducing sales and reputations;
- smuggling reduces the market for legitimate goods and the collection of excise duties;
- illegal immigrants have no employment rights and must work for whatever they are offered – destroying local jobs and standards of living;
- virtual slave labour drives down costs of commodities and makes it hard for legitimate businesses to compete.

The turnover of international crime is now so vast that it has to be considered as a key global issue alongside the economic and environmental issues which present major challenges for the twenty-first century.

6 The trade cycle, unemployment and economic growth

6.1 The trade cycle

Economists define the trade cycle as a period of prosperity, followed by a period of depression, separated by transitional periods of downturn and upturn.

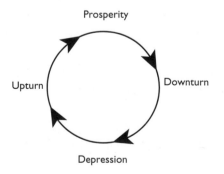

In principle, the idea is hardly new – the Biblical seven lean years following seven fat years is thousands of years old, but very similar in concept.

The trade cycle is much easier to theorize about than to measure. It is like high or low morale, which is easy to recognize when you see it but difficult to quantify.

Certainly, the Great Depression of 1929–1933 was easy enough to recognize, with massive unemployment, bank and business failures, and tangible poverty on the streets of countries in several continents. It followed the boom of 1925–1929, when it had seemed impossible for share prices ever to fall again and you simply had to keep on buying.

If the trade cycle really lasts for ten years, as some economists have argued, then the world has gone through seven cycles between 1932 and 2002. They were punctuated by the upheavals of World War Two (1939–1945) and many other smaller wars, in Korea, Vietnam, Iran/Iraq, the Balkans, Falkland Islands, the Middle East and many countries in Africa.

All of these wars have distorted the picture and make it impossible to draw a neat picture showing the peaks and troughs of the last 70 years.

> J.K. Galbraith, the American economist who lived through the Great Depression and saw the Internet bubble burst 70 years later, said: 'Show me an economic genius and I'll show you a rising market'.

A common factor does seem to be that, during boom years, unrealistic expectations are raised. Share prices increase, people sell them to other people who buy at a higher price in the expectation that prices will rise yet more, and so they do – until confidence, the key word in all economics, evaporates like a morning mist in August – and bust follows.

Meanwhile, underlying trading profits, those essential lubricants of economic activity which many of you work to help produce, decline and are ignored until it is clear that no one is making a return on their investment. Share price inflation can then be seen for what it is – a bubble of gas fuelled by the oxygen of get-rich-quick investors, encouraged by foolhardy advisors – or worse, advisors driven by the prospect of lucrative commissions.

In the real world, politicians, business and trades union leaders in many countries have laboured long and with some success to mitigate the effects of the trade cycle. In particular, they have tried to lessen the distance between the peaks and troughs and make the slopes of the upturns and downturns less steep.

6.2 Unemployment

Rising unemployment is a classic sign of economic downturn. High unemployment is associated with depression, and its opposite with prosperity.

In any economy, no matter how healthy it may be, there will be a level of unemployment.

Inevitably, some companies close or contract in size. Some people simply decide to change their job or move to another part of the country and take a while to find a job there. There can be any number of reasons for unemployment.

Real problems arise when there is high long-term employment which becomes a fact of economic life (often called **structural unemployment**). It may happen in relation to a particular area of a country or, worse still, to the whole of a country, with the risk of political turmoil.

6.3 Economic growth

Promoting economic growth has been one of the primary aims of successive UK Governments in conjunction with policies aimed at controlling inflation and avoiding structural unemployment.

Most people would agree that growth is a desirable objective. Children, young animals, plants and trees are all expected to grow as a part of the natural order of things, so it is natural to think in such terms. In all these cases it is obvious that growth is taking place, but how do you encourage the economy to grow, and how do you recognize economic growth – or the reverse – when you see it?

Encouraging growth

If you think back to the factors of production, you will realize that growth is about:

- stimulating investment in capital;
- making labour more productive.

So it is generally agreed that to promote growth, a government needs to:

- encourage nett savings (which are then invested in productive activities);
- encourage increased productivity among the workforce.

The third factor of production, land, is effectively a fixed resource unless you can reclaim it from the sea.

If you think for a moment about the two stimulants to growth (savings and productivity), it is obvious that they will not always be compatible with other economic objectives.

Activity 80 · 8 mins

Imagine that productivity in an engineering company making buses and coaches improves by 10% as a result of investment in more automated production lines. The company can now make 110 buses in the same time it formerly took to make 100.

What effect might this have on:

1 unemployment, assuming that the market for buses cannot be expanded and unemployment is running at around 8% nationally?

_____

_____

2 inflation, assuming that the employees' pay is increased by 8% and the market for buses can be expanded to take all the extra production? Assume that inflation, as normally reported, is running at 2.4%.

_____

_____

You most probably concluded that:

1 it is likely that some people will lose their jobs. They may take some time to find suitable alternative employment with unemployment already 3% higher than the current UK figure (2002);

2 as people are receiving pay rises well above the rate of inflation, they will have extra spending power – which may lead to demand pull inflation.

Of course, if either event were happening in just one factory, the effects on the UK's vast economy would be tiny. But if they applied to a significant sector of the economy, or in labour-intensive sectors such as teaching, medicine, public services or local/central government, they could have a significant effect on the economy as a whole. For example, replacing large numbers of teachers with technology-based teaching could create significant unemployment; awarding above-inflation pay rises to specific groups of workers could contribute to rising inflation levels when they begin to spend their increased pay.

Again, if people receiving the pay rises chose to spend a high proportion of the rise on overseas travel, or buy second homes in Florida or Spain, that would have an adverse effect on the balance of payments, which in turn could threaten the value of sterling and increase the price of essential imports such as food. As Table (b) in Extension 5 shows, the UK already has a food trade deficit of more than £8,000,000,000 per year. A 5% fall in the value of sterling could add a staggering £400,000,000 to that vast bill.

6.4 Conclusion

By and large, the UK has avoided the worst excesses of economic mismanagement and has one of the most stable systems of government in the world. Whether it continues to do so depends on its citizens. In a democratic system, governments ultimately are elected by the voters and can govern only with their consent.

Governments of every political party face the same problems of reconciling often unrealistic desires with the practical needs of prudent government – and their desire to be re-elected.

The table below contrasts some of the competing desires of the electorate with the competing needs for good government.

Desires of electorate	Needs of government
Ever-improving standards of material prosperity	Keep inflation under control and maintain international competitiveness
Lower taxes	Maintain public services and defence
Full employment, or something approaching it	Prevent wage driven inflation and maintain mobility of labour
Spend your money as you wish	Protect the value of the £ sterling
Ever-increasing expectations of health service, education and social services	Keep taxes to a level which the electorate will tolerate

John Stuart Mill, the nineteenth-century economist and writer said in his *Essay on Liberty*: 'The worth of a state, in the long run, is the worth of the individuals composing it'.

It seems an appropriate thought with which to end this session.

Self-assessment 6 ·

20 mins

1　Underline from the following list **three** examples of items which would increase the UK's imports, assuming that all the purchasers are UK residents:

- buying a meal in a restaurant in Brussels
- paying a train fare to travel from London to Edinburgh
- buying a bottle of German wine in a local supermarket
- sending flowers via the Internet to a relative who lives in Malaysia
- travelling to Florida on a British Airways flight.

2　The balance of _____ measures the overall difference between the UK's _____ and _____, including _____ or 'intangible' items.

3　Increases in the exchange rate of sterling against other currencies makes _____ goods and the cost of _____ travel _____ expensive.

4　Decreases in the exchange rate of sterling against other currencies makes _____ goods more _____ and _____ the costs of items such as overseas _____ rooms and fares on foreign _____.

5　The EU has endeavoured to provide _____ of movement for _____ and goods, a single _____ and political _____ for its member states.

6　_____ who sit in the _____ Parliament are the only people elected to any of the EU's key _____.

7　Give four examples of multinational corporations, including ones which affect your own organization directly or indirectly.

_____

_____

_____

_____

8   What are the four stages of the trade cycle?

_____

_____

_____

_____

9   Underline the correct answer:

Structural unemployment occurs when:

■ people decide to change jobs or move to another part of the country;
■ people in large numbers cannot get jobs for many months or years;
■ some companies close or contract in size.

10   Symptoms of economic contraction include full order books, high levels of savings and investment, and low unemployment.

Do you agree with this statement? Give your reasons.

_____

_____

_____

11   The near universal use of the _____ language makes it relatively simple to move _____ of many kinds from developed to _____ developed countries.

Answers to these questions can be found on pages 204–5.

7 Summary

- The UK's prosperity depends on its continuing ability to trade successfully with the rest of the world in its entirety.

- No one owes us a living, and increasing expenditure on health, education and social provisions generally must be paid for in the long term by economic activity.

- The continuing deficits on visible trade and balance of payments are a concern and could eventually put real pressure on the value of the pound sterling.

- The European Union (EU) began life in 1952 in the desire to end a century of warfare in Europe, especially involving economic disputes between France and Germany. By 2002, there had been 50 years of relative peace since the EU's inception.

- Further EU expansion from the 2002 membership of 15 countries is underway.

- The UK is a member of international organizations which contribute to and distribute aid to poorer countries.

- Globalization is not really a new phenomenon, but the motives of international corporations appear to be distrusted widely, despite the measurable economic contribution which they make to many countries, including the UK.

- International crime now operates on such a vast scale that it can influence the economic affairs of even the largest economies.

- The boom to bust characteristics of previous trade cycles were always associated with unrealistic expectations of ever-rising share prices unrelated to real profits.

- Economic growth needs to be managed to avoid it leading to increasing inflation, unemployment and pressure on exchange rates.

- Countries such as Brazil and Argentina show just how badly and quickly things can go wrong when confidence in a currency is lost.

- The graphic examples of economic contraction in former USSR states show starkly the perils of centralized control which ignores what the market actually demands of an economy.

- Governments of all parties in the UK are constantly trying to reconcile ever-increasing demand for public services with the electorate's unwillingness to pay for them.

- The UK's long-term prosperity depends on political stability and the ingenuity, efficiency and good sense of its people.

Performance checks

▪ 1 Quick quiz

Jot down the answers to the following questions on *Understanding Organizations in their Context.*

Question 1   List five types of organizations that remain, or had their origins in, the voluntary and self help sectors.

_____

_____

Question 2   People will often find their way around rigid organizational structures, from the best of intentions. Can you suggest some ways in which they do so?

_____

_____

_____

Question 3   Complete the following sentence with a suitable phrase selected from the list below.

It is unwise for any business to risk too much time and money in starting a business venture in a market sector that has _____.

a high profit potential
b a low barrier to entry
c several organizations already operating in it
d strict legal requirements as to product safety

Question 4   One of the following documents sets out the way in which a limited company must manage its affairs between the board of directors and the shareholders. Which of the following is it:

a its mission statement;
b the Memorandum of Association;
c the Articles of Association?

_____

Question 5   Complete the following sentence.
Hierarchies with _____ tiers of _____ tend to be _____ to _____ to _____ circumstances and so may be too _____ in a _____ changing business environment, whereas 'wheel' organizations may place _____ _____ responsibility on a single _____ _____.

Question 6   Name the four ways in which money is said to be used.

_____

_____

_____

_____

Question 7   What are the three reasons why a business keeps accounting records and which are reflected in a balance sheet?

_____

_____

_____

Question 8   Name a financial statement which helps an organization plan for the future.

_____

Question 9   Explain how profit is calculated.

_____

_____

Question 10   How is capital used in a business?

_____

_____

Question 11   Give the name for items purchased and kept in an organization for a long period. They are not intended for resale.

_____

Question 12   Explain what is meant by the term debtors.

_____

_____

_____

_____

Question 13   Define working capital.

_____

Question 14   How can an organization anticipate when it will need to borrow money?

_____

_____

Question 15   Explain what is meant by depreciation.

_____

_____

_____

Question 16   What is the profit and loss account of a charity normally called?

_____

_____

Question 17   Define capital employed.

_____

_____

Question 18   Write down the acid test calculation.

_____

_____

_____

Question 19   What is measured by the profit margin?

_____

_____

Question 20   What is meant by ROCE?

_____

_____

Question 21   State a source of both short-term and long-term funds.

_____

_____

_____

_____

Question 22   Allocate the following items to one of the three factors of production.

- garage forecourt
- sheep pasture
- garage mechanic
- airline pilot

- delivery vehicle
- computer programmer
- industrial robot
- bulldozer

- power station
- development site
- stagehand
- airfield

Land	Labour	Capital

Question 23   Land in the UK is some of the most _____ land in the world because of the UK's _____ population _____.

Question 24   Give three examples of the way in which labour may be rewarded, other than through wages and salary payments.

_____

_____

_____

Question 25   Why is it essential for countries to achieve stable economic conditions over extended periods of time?

_____

_____

_____

_____

Question 26   The loss of confidence in a country's _____, the management of its economy or the _____ of its business leaders can quickly destroy its prosperity and create political and civil unrest.

Question 27   The balance of _____ trade shows the monetary difference between what the UK _____ and_____ in visible/ physical or 'tangible' goods.

Question 28   In the following list underline three items which would reduce the UK's balance of payments deficit.

- relocating a call centre formerly operated in Aberdeen to New Delhi
- charging interest on a loan made by a UK bank to a Dutch shipping company
- increasing the number of American visitors to the UK by 5%
- replacing English coal-fired power stations with more efficient ones fuelled with gas from Norwegian oil and gas fields
- increasing the number of UK citizens who take holidays in Scotland, rather than going to other European countries
- equipping the new House of Commons members' facilities with furniture made from Brazilian hardwoods

Question 29   _____ is not a new phenomenon, and many _____ countries have benefited from the activities of organizations which operate globally.

Question 30   What two things must a government do to promote economic growth? What may be the consequences of growth which is too rapid?

_____

_____

_____

_____

_____

Answers to these questions can be found on pages 211–13.

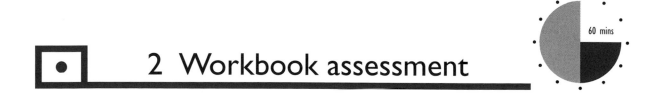

2 Workbook assessment

Read the following case study and then deal with the questions which follow, writing your answers on a separate sheet of paper.

Mike Carlisle and Shidu Razan left the electrical engineering company in North London for which they worked to go into partnership with their own business, trading as Enlightened Enterprises, manufacturing table lamps in a rented industrial unit. Shidu had contacts in the Middle East and they soon began to export a proportion of their output in addition to selling to local hardware and lighting shops with whom they had prudently established contact before setting out on their own. Mike's sister, Frances, sorted out the complex export documentation for them and looked after the accounts. They manufactured to recognized British Standards and instituted a quality system of their own based on ISO 9000 procedures, though they did not go to a formal, externally assessed system. The business grew steadily in the first few months.

After about a year they were approached by a multiple retailer who had become aware of their products and thought them very good. They were offered a substantial contract to supply lamps via a distribution warehouse in Rugby. About half the lamps were going to European stores. Though they had to spend money on equipment and larger premises, and recruit and train new staff, they decided it was an excellent opportunity. The lamps were supplied subject to three months' written notice on either side.

All went well for three years and the multiple business reached 80% of their total sales. Their own export business stayed much the same after the first year, mainly because they had no time to pursue it while meeting the demands of their major customer. At the beginning of March, a letter arrived from their major customer saying that they had found an alternative source of lamps at substantially lower cost. Their stores in Europe were to close, as had been announced in the press. By the terms of the contract, this letter was to give them three months' formal notice. Purchases would be scaled down in anticipation of the European closure which reflected the high price of sterling purchases.

Shidu and Mike found themselves staring disaster in the face. They had invested heavily, and now employed 16 staff on UK-level salaries and employment terms. They had recently borrowed money from the bank to buy new equipment and had contracted to rent another factory unit. Shidu, who owned his own houses, having inherited it from his grandmother, had guaranteed the loan by using his house as security. They now learnt that they were to lose 40% of their business immediately and a further 40% in three months' time. A phone call to one of their immediate contacts revealed that the new suppliers were in China and the Philippines.

In the light of their experience:

- What factors of production have the partners employed?
- How will working as a partnership affect their liability?
- As the two friends are partners, they own the business equally, but Shidu is the only one with any personal asset. How will this affect them if the business goes into liquidation, owing money?
- What legal and international factors have influenced their situation?

Reflect and review

This is an appropriate time to review the objectives set for *Understanding Organizations in their Context.*

When you have completed this workbook, you will be better able to do the following.

■   Describe the forms that organizations can take, the functions required to maintain them and the proper roles of managers at various levels within them.

Do you now have a clear picture of the various forms of organization, and the advantages and drawbacks each form may have? Are you clear about the support that they need from specialist functions, and the true role of managers in supporting, rather than bearing down upon, their staff? Can you relate the principles to your own organization and immediate situation?

■   Distinguish between different organizational structures and their 'fitness for purpose' in differing situations.

Can you now recognize different structures and the organizational purposes that they will help achieve? Is it clear that there is no one structure which will serve all purposes, and that the structure must match the purpose of the organization? Does the structure of your own employer's organization match the purposes that it is supposed to help achieve?

■ Understand how important it is for any organization to have sufficient cash.

Accountants seem to talk of everything as if it were money. Can you see the good reasons for putting a money value on all things and activities in your place of work and generate financial information? As a first line manager, you may be involved in bringing the fixed assets into operation and in using working capital. Are all these used in the most efficient way? Can you think of improvements you can suggest to your manager?

■ Appreciate why it is vital for an organization to control its finances by forecasting and monitoring cash flow.

You may or may not have access to invoices, credit notes and receipts in your day to day work, but hopefully as a first line manager you can encourage your work team to be careful in preserving and passing on whatever source documentation does come your way. Perhaps you can also ensure that cash is not wasted by making sure that your work team minimizes waste.

■ Identify appropriate providers of finance in given situations.

Try to find out how your organization funds short-term shortfalls in finance, and how new long-term projects are funded. What sort of return is made on all the funds used? Does this return vary depending on the type of finance? For instance, shareholders are often willing to take reduced dividends in return for retained profits being used to increase the value of the shares themselves over the medium and long term. Do you think the organization could make better use of the sources of funds that are available to it?

■ Make sense of key financial information in profit and loss accounts and balance sheets.

Think of a major change in your workplace which has been made recently. In general terms, can you see how this might affect the profit and loss account (or income and expenditure account) and balance sheet of your organization?

■ Measure how well an organization is performing financially.

Take a look at the accounts of your business for the last couple of years and calculate the working capital and acid test ratios. What do these tell you about the trend between the two balance sheet dates? Has there been any changes in policy which are likely to have led to the trend. If the position has been constant, is the level appropriate to the type of organization?

■ List the fundamental factors of production and be able to relate them to your own organization and everyday working life.

Do you now have a clear understanding of the basic factors of production? Is it clear that they are used by every organization in some combination to produce goods and services?

■ Outline the eternal economic problems and the limited range of political measures available to tackle them.

Governments have a limited range of levers available, which you have had chance to examine. What will you do with the knowledge you have gained and how will you keep up to date, both personally and in the context of your organization and wider economic events?

■ Recognize the important economic and political factors which affect your organization.

This book should have both confirmed and expanded your knowledge of the way in which political and economic events in this country and overseas influence the work of your organization, whatever business it is involved in.

■ Explain the effect of currency exchange rates on organizations in all countries.

A reduction in the value of a currency always has serious consequences for a country, making essential imports expensive and undermining confidence in the local economy. The UK has never experienced a collapse in the value of sterling, though there have been devaluations, and the pound has depreciated over many years against the US dollar. How will you now try to monitor the effects of fluctuations in exchange rates on your organization and its situation in the economy?

■ Describe the structure of the EU and its impact on the UK and its business.

Do you understand the structure and operations of the EU clearly and the impact which it has had in changing the UK's way of running its affairs? Is it clear what affect the EU has on your own organization's operations? How will you maintain a continuing interest to enable you to enter into an informed debate over issues such as the potential entry of the UK into the Eurozone and the proposed continuing expansion of EU membership?

■ Identify the influences beyond the EU which are significant for UK business.

Do you have a clearer understanding of the global issues facing your own organization and UK businesses and general standards of living? Have you developed some ideas which could help to meet the challenges? How will you be taking a continuing interest in matters which affect everyone in the UK, but are often ignored by the mass media?

■ Outline the effect which the globalization of business has on local organizations throughout the world.

Organizations which operate globally are often much larger than the economies of developing countries and have no electorate to answer to. Many such companies operate in the UK and some global companies are also based here. Do you now have a better understanding of the scope and potential impact of such organizations generally, and as they affect your own organization's activities?

2 Action plan

Use this plan to further develop for yourself a course of action you want to take. Make a note in the left-hand column of the issues or problems you want to tackle, and then decide what you want to do, and make a note in column 2.

The resources you need might include time, materials, information or money. You may need to negotiate for some of them, but others could be easy to acquire, like half an hour of somebody's time, or a chapter of a book. Put whatever you need in column 3. No plan means anything without a timescale, so put a realistic target completion date in column 4.

Desired outcomes							
I Issues	2 Action		3 Resources		4 Target completion		
Actual outcomes							

◉ 3 Extensions

MISSION STATEMENT
ALPHA & OMEGA plc
Always first and built to last

This Company intends to use world-class manufacturing and management practices to assure the best interests of all the recognized stakeholders in our business: customers, employees and former employees, suppliers, the local community and the wider environment.

About customers

We are determined to exceed our customers' expectations of us regarding products and services at all times. In our business, the customer is truly the king.

About employees

Employees are our most valuable resource. We will ensure that all our employees achieve contentment in their work and do not regard any as just 'another employee'. If an employee has a problem, then it is as much our problem than his or hers. We will continue our concern for welfare through into the retirement years of our former employees.

About suppliers

We believe in promoting partnership with our suppliers and developing long-term relationships with them to the mutual benefit of both parties. This we extend to overseas suppliers in countries where our business is vital to the local economy.

About our neighbours and the environment

We have regard always to the potential impact of our activities on the local community and the wider environment and use every endeavour to eliminate any adverse effects that we might produce in either.

Graham Bowmond, Chief Executive Officer

Extension 2

Book	*Business Accounting*
Authors	Alan Sangster and Frank Wood
Edition	2002
Publisher	Pearson Education

Extension 3

Some UK regulatory bodies and legal measures used by the UK Government

Companies Acts 1948–1998

A succession of Acts has regulated the way in which companies behave, and amendments are made as practices formerly acceptable become less so, or governments discover other ways in which the letter and spirit of earlier legislation is being flouted.

In particular, the Acts regulate:

■ the issue of prospectuses inviting the public to subscribe for shares;
■ what a company can and cannot do under its certificate of incorporation;
■ how the authority to manage its affairs is to be divided between the shareholders and directors;
■ directors' powers to raise capital.

It is very necessary to have close regulation of limited liability companies. They are treated as having an identity in law separate from their owners and managers, unlike a sole trader or members of a partnership. This continues to cause difficulty, for example, in knowing whom (if anyone) to prosecute for manslaughter following disasters such as rail crashes where lives are lost and where the business is operated by a limited liability company.

Competition Act 1998

This law, akin to that which is used in Europe to check organizations exploiting a dominant monopolistic position enjoyed by a number of co-operating suppliers, for example, in professions such as architecture and accountancy. The law is enforced by the Director General of Fair Trading, and a new Competition Commission has been established to succeed the Monopolies and Mergers Commission.

Restrictive Trade Practices Acts 1956–1976

This legislation outlaws practices concerned with price fixing between ostensibly competing suppliers. The law is enforced by the Restrictive Practices Court. Suppliers have in the past tried both to maintain prices at levels higher than competition would allow and to prevent retailers selling products below the price they have set, for example, by collectively withdrawing supplies. The 1976 Act extends the scope of the legislation to include service agreements.

Resale Prices Act 1964

This Act forbids manufacturers to set minimum recommended prices for their goods or to enforce such prices through sanctions such as lower discounts to sellers who ignore the recommended price levels. There are exemptions in the case of books which still apply in 2002. Currently, there are often recommended retail prices, which are in effect **maximum** prices, rather than the **minimum** prices set by organizations before the abolition of resale price maintenance.

Fair Trading Act 1973

This Act established the office of Director General of Fair Trading to adjudicate in cases of monopoly. Monopoly is more stringently defined as being a 25% share of the market (formerly 33%). Proposed mergers which have monopolistic implications can be referred to the Director General for adjudication. The existence of this legislation acts as a deterrent to companies that may have less than honourable reasons for wishing to merge.

Competition Commission (formerly the Monopolies and Mergers Commission)

As its name implies, the Competition Commission is charged with looking into a wide range of practices which restrict competition and to decide whether any public interest is served by such practices. Company directors can be ingenious at finding ways of co-operating to flout the spirit of the law, even if they are seemingly obeying its letter. This makes the Commission's task very hard. The welter of information involved in large company operations and the spin which can be put on the facts to support a case on whose success may depend billions of pounds can make it virtually impossible to see the true position.

Financial Services Authority (FSA)

The FSA was established in 1997 and is charged with overseeing the activities of the financial sector, including banking, insurance, pensions, building societies and companies trading in securities. The FSA has not been viewed as an unqualified success but, given the complexities of intangible financial products such as endowment policies and unit trusts, it is hardly surprising that it is difficult for **any** body to keep watch over such a complex field.

Extension 4

Title: *Annual Abstract of Statistics*
Publisher: The Stationery Office
Edition: 2002

Extension 5   Some UK trading figures

Table (a) Imports and exports – total figures
(all figures given in £ billions)

Balance of visible trade	1997	1998	1999	2000	2001
Goods exported (a)	172	164	166	188	191
Goods imported (b)	184	185	193	218	224
Surplus/(deficit) (c) = (a) + (b)	(12)	(21)	(27)	(30)	(33)
Cumulative deficit	(12)	(33)	(60)	(90)	(123)
Invisible items surplus/(deficit) **(d)**	10	16	8	13	13
Balance of payments	(2)	(5)	(19)	(17)	(20)
surplus/(deficit) (e) = (c) − (d)					
Cumulative deficit	(2)	(7)	(26)	(43)	(63)

Table (b) Visible trade by type (2000)

Category	Imports (a)		Exports (b)		Surplus/(deficit) (a) – (b) £ billion
	£ billion	% of total	£ billion	% of total	
Machinery/vehicles	99.2	46	87.6	47	(11.6)
Manufactured goods	32.8	15	21.2	11	(11.6)
Manufactured materials	29.3	13	22.7	12	(6.6)
Chemicals, oils, fats	21.0	9	25.1	14	4.1
Food, drink, tobacco	18.0	8	9.9	5	(8.1)
Fuels	9.9	5	17.1	9	7.2
Raw materials	5.8	3	2.4	1	(3.4)
Miscellaneous	1.8	1	1.7	1	(0.1)
Totals	217.8	100	187.9	100	(30.0)

Table (c) UK imports and exports (2000)
£ billion – in descending order of UK exports

Country	Exports	Imports	Surplus/(deficit)
USA	29.4	28.5	0.9
Germany	22.7	27.7	(5.0)
France	18.5	18.2	0.3
Netherlands	15.1	15.1	0
Republic of Ireland	12.3	9.5	2.8
Belgium	10.3	11.6	(1.3)
Italy	8.4	9.4	(1.0)
Spain	8.3	6.0	2.3
Oil exporting countries	6.1	4.3	1.8
Sweden	4.2	4.9	(0.7)
Japan	3.7	10.2	(6.5)
Canada	3.5	4.0	(0.5)
Switzerland	3.1	5.5	(2.4)
Australia	2.7	1.5	1.2
Hong Kong	2.7	5.9	(3.2)
India	2.1	1.7	0.4
China	1.5	4.8	(3.3)
South Korea	1.4	3.4	(2.0)
Taiwan	1.0	3.6	(2.6)
Russia	0.7	1.5	(0.8)
Other countries	30.3	40.7	(10.4)
Totals	188	218	(30)

Extension 6   Some factors which give the USA economic advantage

Land:

- large land mass, relatively lightly populated;
- low costs of land in most areas for farming and industry;
- forms virtually an island, free of major threats on its borders with Canada and Mexico;
- few land borders; position encourages trade across both Pacific and Atlantic Oceans;
- varied climate, allowing growth of virtually any crop and every sort of holiday.

Labour:

- experienced, skilled workforce in many disciplines. Flexibility in working practices is common;
- has strong scientific base in all disciplines;
- expertise in production engineering and information technology;
- stable political system; commitment by large majority to a single cultural identity. Freedom from general war on its land mass since end of Civil War (1861–1865);
- until recently, English has been common language throughout entire population and the language of commerce almost everywhere.

Capital:

- vast industrial base developed over 100 years or more. Home to many multi-national corporations;
- military and space research have driven technological development;
- highly developed communications infrastructure by every means;
- common currency throughout all states, enormous reserves of gold and foreign currency, no tariff barriers within whole vast economy;
- educational system developed over more than a century.

Resources:

- vast natural resources, including those in Alaska;
- food abundant, though some major imports – including coffee.

Extension 7   The European Union

Member states (2006)

Austria	Belgium	Bulgaria	Cyprus	Czech Republic
Denmark	Estonia	Finland	France	Germany
Greece	Hungary	Ireland	Italy	Latvia
Lithuania	Luxembourg	Malta	Poland	Portugal
Romania	Slovakia	Slovenia	Spain	Sweden
The Netherlands	United Kingdom			

The Treaty of Nice allows any European State with a proven democratic form of government to apply for membership and Turkey, which is chiefly in Asia, has also applied to join.

No country is allowed to join the EU unless it can prove to the existing members' satisfaction that it is a democracy.

4 Answers to self-assessment questions

Self-assessment 1 on pages 34–5

1 The sign of a **good/well run** organization is that the **whole** is **greater** than the sum of its parts.

2 **Excellent management communications** is the basis for continuing success in any successful organization in the long term.

3 Investing in a company's shares removes from investors the threat of **unlimited personal liability**.

4 Among the disadvantages that partnerships share with sole traders are unlimited personal liability; difficulty in raising substantial sums of money; difficulty in organizing succession as original personnel changes.

5 Becoming a franchisee is now popular as a way of starting, or expanding, a business because it provides a private individual, or fairly small organization, with the marketing 'clout' of a powerful brand – **provided** they choose the right franchising organization.

6 The two kinds of limited liability company are Private Limited and Public Limited Companies. The latter is often abbreviated to 'plc' and can, unlike a 'private' company, sell its shares to unlimited numbers of shareholders via the stock exchange.

7 Neither limited companies, nor registered charities, can do anything legally other than what is covered by the objectives that they state when they register.

8 One of the principal differences between a public sector and a private sector organization is that the former is a **cost centre** whereas the latter is a **profit centre**.

9 When considering a major **reorganization** of their **activity**, senior managers should bear in mind the maxim 'that no **profit** is generated inside a **business**, only **cost**'.

Self-assessment 2 on pages 63–5

1   In simple terms, companies keep accounting records to show what they own, owe and are owed. So suitable words would be:

a OWES to other people;
b OWED by other people;
c OWNS.

On the basis of these accounting records, the company can adjust what it is doing, so that it continues to make a profit and can plan what the business should do next. So the final responses should be along the lines of:

d PAID OUT to other people;
e PLAN for the future.

2   The following match and show money being used as:

a a medium of exchange, when (i) buying a bus ticket;
b a store of wealth, when (iii) contributing to a pension plan;
c a means of deferred payment, when (iv) buying a coat using a credit card;
d a measure of value, when having (ii) an antique clock valued at £750.

3   a The surplus or profit of an organization is calculated by using the formula:

Profit = Total income − Total expenditure

b Your two reasons why a business needs to make a profit could be selected from:

■ to survive;
■ to grow;
■ to reward investors and owners;
■ to replace machinery, equipment and so on.

4   a Information on transactions in source documents is recorded in accounting records. These are then summarized in accounts, which allow the enterprise to see whether it is making a profit or surplus, and achieving its plans.

b 1 Goods (net) total, VAT, invoice (gross) total, date/tax point.
    2 The same.
    3 The amount of the cheque.

5 The items are matched as follows:

a Owner's capital   (ii)   Capital provided by the business owner.
b Fixed assets   (i)   Assets used within the business, and not intended for resale.
c Working capital   (v)   Current assets less current liabilities.
d Labour   (vi)   The cost to the business of its employees.
e Overheads   (vii) The incidental expenses incurred in running a business, including fuel and rent.
f Debtors   (iv)   People who owe the business money.
g Creditors   (iii) People the business owes money to.

6 The most straightforward way to answer this question is to draw up a cash flow forecast.

	May £	June £
Opening capital	450	–
Receipts from sales	1,040	990
Receipts	1,490	990
Materials paid for	(500)	(560)
Overheads	(200)	(210)
Payments	(700)	(770)
Net cash	790	220
Balance B/F	Nil	790
Balance C/F	790	1,010

There is just enough money to buy the van for £1,000 but that would mean leaving the business very short of cash. Julia might be well advised to wait a little longer before making her purchase. Alternatively she could try to borrow money towards the cost of the delivery van which she could pay off over a longer period.

7 Offering customers a six month interest free credit period after previously allowing customers only one month credit means that the business will need to wait an extra five months for receipt for sales, and so will need to finance roughly five extra months' debtors. It is difficult to quantify this exactly, as some customers might not want to take up the offer and others might pay earlier than the six month period. In addition the business will be expecting the level of sales to increase so it will have to buy more stock to meet increased orders.

Together these factors will mean increased pressure on working capital with the figures for both stock and debtors increasing. Some of this may be offset by negotiating longer credit periods from suppliers, but the remaining squeeze on working capital will need to be financed. This may well mean negotiating an overdraft to tide the business over.

The benefits of making an offer like this are that the business is likely to generate more sales with existing and new customers which, providing all customers pay for what they order, means an increase in profits.

Self-assessment 3 on pages 92–4

1 The profit and loss account should be as follows:

Lester Limited

Profit and loss account for the year ended 31 December

	£'000	£'000
Sales (352 + 400)		752
Cost of goods sold (20 + 520 − 70)		(470)
Gross profit		282
Overhead expenses		
Expenses	120	
Interest	12	
Depreciation	40	(172)
Profit before tax		110
Tax (110 × 20%)		(22)
Profit after tax		88
Dividend		(4)
Retained profit for the year		£84

---

2 a Assets that are to be kept and used in the business are FIXED assets.

b Assets that are expected to be turned into cash very soon are CURRENT assets.

Current assets are separated from fixed assets because a company needs to know how much cash it has, including items that it expects shortly to turn into cash.

So current assets are actual cash, plus goods for sale, money owed to the business, and so on, that will soon be turned into cash.

3   The items are described as follows:

    a Working capital is (ii) current assets less current liabilities.

    b Capital employed is (iv) long-term liabilities and owner's funds.

    c Depreciation is the (iii) amount written off the value of a fixed asset.

    d Balance sheet is a (i) statement in which assets equal liabilities.

4    $\dfrac{£240,000}{£400,000} = 0.6{:}1.$

5    $\dfrac{£240,000 - £120,000}{£400,000} = \dfrac{£120,000}{£400,000} = 0.3{:}1.$

6    $\text{Profit margin} = \dfrac{\text{Profit before tax}}{\text{Sales revenue}} \times 100$

7   Profit and loss account.

8   Look back at the ratio for previous years, and compare the ratio with other companies. You may also be able to compare it against an 'industry standard'.

9    $\text{Return on capital employed} = \dfrac{\text{Profit before tax}}{\text{Capital employed}} \times 100$

10   Look at the balance sheet, work out the total assets and take away liabilities other than the owner's capital and reserves.

11   A cash flow forecast, where forecast figures are compared with actual figures, illustrates how successfully an organization is being run, particularly when meeting its debts.

12   Different types of business and organization typically have different ratios; it is meaningless to compare the performance of businesses in widely different industries.

Self-assessment 4 on pages 104

1   a Types of short-term finance include bank overdraft, trade credit or retained profits.

    b Types of long-term finance include share capital, loans, grants or retained profits.

2   The interest rate charged on borrowing is important when deciding how to finance a new project because no project is worth undertaking if it costs more than its potential return. Also, the rate may not be fixed and may increase over the period of the project.

3   Leasing may be a useful source of finance when the machinery or equipment leased can be used to generate money to pay the finance charges when due.

4 Retained profits are a popular source of finance because no interest or dividends are payable on them. They are therefore a cheap source of finance.

5 Homes for the Homeless as a charity is likely to be eligible for grants to help them renovate the houses. As charities are non-profit organizations, they must rely on donations for their other finance needs. Some income will be provided by the low rents but this is unlikely to be enough to pay back the cost of property and renovation in a short period.

Self-assessment 5 on pages 146–7

1 The three factors of production are:

- land;
- labour;
- capital.

2 Organizations may strive to become 'least cost producer' in their fields:

- to protect themselves against overseas competition;
- to retain business in the face of demands for lower prices from their customers.

3 The non-renewable resources listed are natural gas, coal, crude oil and iron ore.

4 Other things being equal, the more **ABUNDANT/SCARCE** a factor of production becomes, the **LOWER/HIGHER** will be its **MARKET** price.

5 If the cost of labour becomes relatively **HIGH/EXPENSIVE**, organizations will seek to **REPLACE** it with **CAPITAL** equipment, or by finding people prepared to **WORK FOR LOWER RATES**

6 Monopoly arises where a single supplier or co-operating group of suppliers control the production and/or distribution of goods or services and so can fix prices to suit themselves.

7 Subsidies can distort the price mechanism and cause suppliers of goods or services to believe that their activities have a higher market price than they would really command. If and when the subsidy is removed, this can lead to a sharp fall in price and unpleasant consequences for the supplier. You may believe that state subsidies can be justified to help disadvantaged sectors of society, here or in other countries.

8 Examples of indirect competition could include:

- for a bus operator in London, Manchester or Newcastle: taxis, tubes, trams;
- for a fish and chip shop: any other fast food outlet, such as Indian or Chinese take-aways;
- for a cinema: live theatre or home entertainments such as TV and home videos.

9 The levying of **DIRECT** taxes, such as income tax and **CORPORATION** tax are examples of the government's **FISCAL** policies in action.

10 Indirect taxes, such as **VAT** and **COUNCIL TAX/EXCISE DUTIES** are deemed to be **REGRESSIVE** because they bear more heavily on people with **LOWER** incomes.

11 Every government's dilemma concerning fiscal policy is that the electorate demand higher and higher levels of **PUBLIC SERVICES**, but are unwilling to see **TAXES** rise to pay for them.

12 Exchange rates measure the relative **PURCHASING** power of two **CURRENCIES** and indicate the **UNDERLYING** strength of their economies.

13 Examples of cost push inflation might include rises in the prices material costs; rents; wage or salary rates; costs of replacing equipment, and increases in rates of VAT which have to be passed on to consumers.

Demand pull shows up clearly when anything is in short supply, as has happened with oil, housing and the prices paid by companies for licences to operate mobile phone systems.

Wage-related inflation has occurred in organizations which rely heavily on the labour factor of production, such as teaching, health provision and the services undertaken by local authorities.

14 Unemployment can arise from causes such as the **DEPLETION** of natural resources, the **REPLACEMENT/SUBSTITUTION** of labour with **CAPITAL** equipment, or the **RELOCATION** of activities elsewhere in pursuit of **CHEAPER** labour.

15 Uncontrolled or **HYPER** inflation inevitably leads to **MASS/HIGH** unemployment, which can **BRING DOWN/DESTABILIZE** governments and lead to **EXTREMIST REGIMES** gaining power.

Self-assessment 6 on pages 177–8

1 Three examples of items which would increase the UK's imports, assuming that all the purchasers are UK residents, are:

■ buying a meal in a restaurant in Brussels;
■ buying a bottle of German wine in a local supermarket;
■ sending flowers via the Internet to a relative who lives in Malaysia.

2 The balance of **PAYMENTS** measures the overall difference between the UK's **IMPORTS** and **EXPORTS**, including **INVISIBLE** or 'intangible items'.

3 Increases in the exchange rate of sterling against other currencies makes **IMPORTED** goods and the cost of **FOREIGN/OVERSEAS** travel **LESS** expensive.

4 Decreases in the exchange rate of sterling against other currencies makes **IMPORTED** goods more **EXPENSIVE** and **INCREASES** the costs of items such as overseas **HOTEL** rooms and fares on foreign **AIRCRAFT/TRAINS**.

5 The EU has endeavoured to provide **FREEDOM** of movement for **PEOPLE** and goods, a single **CURRENCY** and political **STABILITY** for its member states.

6 MEPs who sit in the **EUROPEAN** Parliament are the only people elected to any of the EU's key **INSTITUTIONS**.

7 The answer will vary according to who you work for, but might include Nestlé; Coca Cola; McDonalds; British American Tobacco (BAT), all large oil companies (BP; Texaco; Shell) Glaxo; Monsanto; car manufacturers such as Ford, Nissan, Toyota – as general examples of organizations operating in many countries and often several continents.

8 The normally agreed four stages of the trade cycle are:

- prosperity;
- downturn;
- depression;
- upturn.

9 Structural unemployment occurs when people in large numbers cannot get jobs for many months or years.

10 The statement is incorrect, as these would be symptoms of economic growth.

11 The near universal use of the **ENGLISH** language makes it relatively simple to move **JOBS** of many kinds from developed to **LESS** developed countries.

5 Answers to activities

Activity 8 on page 16

The rewritten sentence should read:
'The purpose of this Company is to manufacture, distribute and sell **any** form of **transportation** for use by individuals or public service operators.'

This gives the company the flexibility it needs to respond to changes in the market.

Activity 9 on page 18

Public sector organizations include the following.

- Hospitals, NHS medical and dentistry services
- Schools, colleges & universities
- Royal Mail
- Government departments – Inland Revenue, Customs & Excise, Social Security
- Police, ambulance service and fire brigades
- The Environment Agency
- Trading standards and regulatory bodies like the Financial Services uthority
- The armed forces and intelligence/anti espionage services

Activity 11 on page 20

Many organizations sprang from poverty and inequality between employers and employees in nineteenth-century Britain and continue to function in the twenty-first century. They include the following.

- Trades Unions.
- Co-operative Societies.
- Building Societies.
- Friendly Societies.
- Mutual Societies.

Activity 16 on page 33

The specialist functions which a modern organization is likely to have are as follows.

1 Finance
2 Marketing/product development
3 Sales
4 Distribution
5 Human resources
6 Production
7 Engineering/Technical
8 Public relations
9 Research
10 Information technology
11 Safety/Environment/Risk management

No order of priority is implied by the list. The names of departments and the mix will vary according to the purpose of the organization.

Activity 18 on pages 40–1

Your completed accounts should look like this:

	What you are owed	What you owe
Monday	£ 60	£ 30
Tuesday	£ 60	£ 35
Wednesday	£ 60	£ 45
Thursday	£ 60	£ 40
Friday	£ 60	£ 10
Saturday	£ nil	£ 20
Sunday	£ nil	£ 10
Totals	£300	£190

Businesses tend to deal in larger sums but the principles are the same.

Activity 37 on page 71

You will probably have arrived at your figure for the cost of goods sold by adding £10,000 opening stock to £20,000 purchases, and taking away the closing stock of £5,000 to get £25,000.

Here is the profit and loss account of Straton Limited:

Straton Limited
Profit and loss account for the year ended 31 March

	£	£
Sales		60,000
Less cost of goods sold		(25,000)
Gross profit		35,000
Labour	15,000	
Overheads	10,000	(25,000)
Net profit		£10,000

Activity 58 on page 112

Land	Capital	Labour
■ development site	■ delivery vehicle	■ itinerant fruit picker
■ agricultural field	■ computer	■ receptionist
■ garage forecourt	■ combine harvester	■ shop worker
■ car park	■ power station	■ managing director
■ riverside wharf	■ video camera	■ economist

Activity 61 on
pages 117–18

Organization	Land	Capital	Labour	Raw materials
Hospital	car park	X ray machine	surgeon	dressings
Call centre	office space	computerized switchboard	customer care assistant	standard letters
Internet marketing company	rented garage	computer	entrepreneur	goods delivery notes
Take-away pizza shop	rented shop	travelling oven	shop assistant	flour and water
Newspaper	print room	high speed press	sub editor	ink
Football club	football pitch	gymnasium	goalkeeper	practice balls

Activity 64 on
page 124

The typical additional on costs which an employer may have to bear are:

1 employer's contribution to National Insurance Fund (NIC)
2 pension contribution
3 holiday pay
4 statutory sick pay
5 maternity leave cover
6 subsidized food/beverages.

Activity 65 on
page 125

The most obvious answer is water. Following privatization, supply was taken over by local profit-making companies who effectively are the only suppliers in an extensive area. Unlike gas, electricity or railway travel, there is no substitute for water and no arrangements have been made for competing companies to use the same supply infrastructure – as happens with BT telephone lines.

The Government has recognized the possible consequences of this effective monopoly and appointed a regulator, OFWAT, to control prices and other aspects of their businesses. It has also removed the right of a supplier to cut off supply to a customer who does not pay – because of the essential nature of water and the public health implications of disconnection.

Activity 72 on page 141

Each unit of local currency is now worth 75/100 pence, or 75 pence. Therefore, to buy the same amount of goods from the UK, the other country must export 100/75, or 1.33 times as much. To sell one third more goods is an enormous task – and what happens if its potential buyer doesn't need or want them?

Activity 74 on page 151

Comparative answer

Imports		Exports	
Invisibles	**Visibles**	**Invisibles**	**Visibles**
Foreign holidays	Tropical fruits and vegetables	Tourism	Meat and meat products
Electricity	Cars and commercial vehicles	Banking services	Steel and construction materials
Shipping	Electrical goods – fridges, etc.	Insurance services	Chemical products – plastics
Civil aviation	Oil and petrol	Airlines' earnings	Tobacco products
Financial services	Clothing and footwear	Shipping	Fuels

Activity 76 on page 159

1 The country we have the largest trade deficit with is Japan, at £6.5 billion.

2 The country we have the largest trade surplus with is the Republic of Ireland, at £2.8 billion.

3 China, Hong Kong, South Korea and Taiwan together account for £11.1 billion of the total UK deficit.

4 As a percentage of the total UK deficit of £30 billion, these four countries account for 37%.

5   The countries with which the UK's trade is approximately in balance are the USA, France, Netherlands, Sweden, Canada, India and Russia. You may have included Italy, with whom we had a deficit of exactly £1 billion.

6   The UK's largest single trading partner is the USA, with £29.4 billion of exports and £28.5 billion of imports – a total trade flow of £57.9 billion.

Activity 77 on pages 160–1

1   The UK's balance of visible trade with Sweden will tend to **worsen** because of the imports from Sweden.

2   Germany's balance of visible trade with Sweden will also tend to **worsen**.

3   UK Exports of visible trade items will **increase** somewhat, assuming that some of the company's 2,000 suppliers are in the UK.

4   Sweden's balance of trade on visible items with China will tend to **worsen** given that many of the company's goods are imported from there.

5   The exchange rate of sterling against the Swedish Krona may depreciate **if** there are more imports of goods from Sweden than exports of goods manufactured here. In any event, the individual effect would be marginal.

Activity 78 on page 168

1   The wine will be worth 30% less, and so to earn the same amount of sterling, the company will have to sell more than 7 million pesos' worth of wine – an enormous increase which is probably unachievable.

2   The fuel will cost around 28.5 million pesos – 8.5 million extra, which will probably have to be passed on to customers at the pumps, if they can afford to pay.

3   Because he both buys and sells in pesos, he would not be directly affected, other factors being equal.

6 Answers to the quick quiz

Answer 1   You might have listed any of the following: Charities; Trades Unions; Mutual and Friendly societies; Building Societies; Co-operative societies; Workers' education societies; Credit Unions; Professional associations and Craft Guilds, amongst others known to you.

Answer 2   People often find their way around rigid organizational structures by using initiative, acting speedily before the organization can find out what they are doing, and by developing their political skills to use unofficial communication channels.

Answer 3   It is unwise for any business to risk too much time and money in starting a business venture in a market sector that has **a low barrier to entry**.

Answer 4   **The Articles of Association** set out the way in which a limited company must manage its affairs as between the board of directors and the shareholders.

Answer 5   Hierarchies with **many** tiers of **management** tend to be **slow** to **react** to **changing** circumstances and so may be too **inflexible** in a **rapidly** changing business environment, whereas 'wheel' organizations may place **too much** responsibility on a single **senior manager/decision-taker**.

Answer 6   The four ways in which money is said to be used are: as a medium of exchange; as a store of wealth, as a means of deferred payment and as a measure of values.

Answer 7   The three reasons why a business keeps accounting records and which are reflected in a balance sheet are to know what it owes, to know what it is owed and to know what it owns.

Answer 8   Cash flow forecast. (Other forecasts can also be used.)

Answer 9   Profit = Total income less total expenditure.

Answer 10   Capital is used to purchase fixed assets and to provide working capital.

Answer 11   Fixed assets.

Answer 12   Debtors refer to the amounts outstanding from customers who are sold goods or services on credit, or to the customers themselves.

Answer 13   Working capital is current assets less current liabilities.

Answer 14   A cash flow forecast indicates when it is necessary to borrow money to meet liabilities.

Answer 15   Depreciation charges the cost of fixed assets to the profit and loss account over time.

Answer 16   An income and expenditure account.

Answer 17   Capital employed is total assets less liabilities **or** owner's capital plus retained profits.

Answer 18 $\text{Acid test} = \dfrac{\text{Current assets} - \text{Stock}}{\text{Current liabilities}}$

Answer 19   The profit margin measures the amount of net profit created from sales and is expressed as a percentage.

Answer 20   Return on capital employed.

Answer 21   Retained profits.

Answer 22

Land	Labour	Capital
■ garage forecourt ■ sheep pasture ■ development site ■ airfield	■ computer programmer ■ garage mechanic ■ stagehand ■ airline pilot	■ delivery vehicle ■ power station ■ industrial robot ■ bulldozer

Answer 23   Land in the UK is some of the most **EXPENSIVE** land in the world because of the UK's **HIGH** population **DENSITY**.

Answer 24   Other ways in which labour may be rewarded include royalties, commission, professional fees, piece work rates and bonuses.

Answer 25   It is essential for countries to achieve stable economic conditions over extended periods of time so that conditions can be created where economic activity can thrive and governments can provide generally acceptable levels of service for health, education and other welfare provision.

Answer 26   The loss of confidence in a country's **CURRENCY**, the management of its economy or the **INTEGRITY** of its business leaders can quickly destroy its prosperity and create political and civil unrest.

Answer 27   The balance of **VISIBLE** trade shows the monetary difference between what the UK **IMPORTS** and **EXPORTS** in visible/physical or 'tangible' goods.

Answer 28   The three items which would reduce the UK's balance of payments deficit are:

- charging interest on a loan made by a UK bank to a Dutch shipping company;
- increasing the number of American visitors to the UK by 5%;
- increasing the number of UK citizens who take holidays in Scotland, rather than going to other European countries.

Answer 29   **GLOBALIZATION** is not a new phenomenon, and many **DEVELOPING** countries have benefited from the activities of organizations which operate globally.

Answer 30   The two things a government must do to promote economic growth are to:

- promote nett savings which flows into capital investment;
- increase the productivity of labour.

The undesirable consequences of growth which is too rapid could include:

- accelerating inflation;
- pressure on the sterling exchange rate.

7 Certificate

Completion of this certificate by an authorized person shows that you have worked through all the parts of this workbook and satisfactorily completed the assessments. The certificate provides a record of what you have done that may be used for exemptions or as evidence of prior learning against other nationally certificated qualifications.

superseries

Understanding Organizations
in their Context

....

has satisfactorily completed this workbook

Name of signatory ....

Position ....

Signature ....

Date ....

Official stamp

Pergamon
Flexible
Learning

Fifth Edition

superseries

FIFTH EDITION

Workbooks in the series:

Achieving Objectives Through Time Management	978-0-08-046415-2
Building the Team	978-0-08-046412-1
Coaching and Training your Work Team	978-0-08-046418-3
Communicating One-to-One at Work	978-0-08-046438-1
Developing Yourself and Others	978-0-08-046414-5
Effective Meetings for Managers	978-0-08-046439-8
Giving Briefings and Making Presentations in the Workplace	978-0-08-046436-7
Influencing Others at Work	978-0-08-046435-0
Introduction to Leadership	978-0-08-046411-4
Managing Conflict in the Workplace	978-0-08-046416-9
Managing Creativity and Innovation in the Workplace	978-0-08-046441-1
Managing Customer Service	978-0-08-046419-0
Managing Health and Safety at Work	978-0-08-046426-8
Managing Performance	978-0-08-046429-9
Managing Projects	978-0-08-046425-1
Managing Stress in the Workplace	978-0-08-046417-6
Managing the Effective Use of Equipment	978-0-08-046432-9
Managing the Efficient Use of Materials	978-0-08-046431-2
Managing the Employment Relationship	978-0-08-046443-5
Marketing for Managers	978-0-08-046974-4
Motivating to Perform in the Workplace	978-0-08-046413-8
Obtaining Information for Effective Management	978-0-08-046434-3
Organizing and Delegating	978-0-08-046422-0
Planning Change in the Workplace	978-0-08-046444-2
Planning to Work Efficiently	978-0-08-046421-3
Providing Quality to Customers	978-0-08-046420-6
Recruiting, Selecting and Inducting New Staff in the Workplace	978-0-08-046442-8
Solving Problems and Making Decisions	978-0-08-046423-7
Understanding Change in the Workplace	978-0-08-046424-4
Understanding Culture and Ethics in Organizations	978-0-08-046428-2
Understanding Organizations in their Context	978-0-08-046427-5
Understanding the Communication Process in the Workplace	978-0-08-046433-6
Understanding Workplace Information Systems	978-0-08-046440-4
Working with Costs and Budgets	978-0-08-046430-5
Writing for Business	978-0-08-046437-4

For prices and availability please telephone our order helpline
or email

+44 (0) 1865 474010
directorders@elsevier.com